RUDOLF STEIN
his spiritual philo
meaning 'wisdom of the human being . As a
highly developed seer, he based his work on
direct knowledge and perception of spiritual dimensions. He initiated a modern and
universal 'science of spirit', accessible to anyone willing to
exercise clear and unprejudiced thinking.

From his spiritual investigations Steiner provided sugges-
tions for the renewal of many activities, including education
(both general and special), agriculture, medicine, economics, architecture, science, philosophy, religion and the
arts. Today there are thousands of schools, clinics, farms and
other organizations involved in practical work based on his
principles. His many published works feature his research
into the spiritual nature of the human being, the evolution of
the world and humanity, and methods of personal development. Steiner wrote some 30 books and delivered over 6000
lectures across Europe. In 1924 he founded the General
Anthroposophical Society, which today has branches
throughout the world.

INTUITION
The Focus of Thinking

RUDOLF STEINER

Compiled and edited by Edward de Boer

RUDOLF STEINER PRESS

Translated by J. Collis

Rudolf Steiner Press
Hillside House, The Square
Forest Row, RH18 5ES

www.rudolfsteinerpress.com

Published by Rudolf Steiner Press 2019

Originally published in German under the title *Intuition, Brennpunkt des Denkens* by Rudolf Steiner Verlag, Basel, in 2014

A catalogue record for this book is available from the British Library

Print book ISBN: 978 1 85584 557 2
Ebook ISBN: 978 1 85584 503 9

Cover by Morgan Creative
Typeset by DP Photosetting, Neath, West Glamorgan
Printed and bound by 4Edge Ltd., Essex

CONTENTS

Introduction

The concept of Intuition is fundamental to Anthroposophy. We meet it in Rudolf Steiner's early writings on Goethe's works, in his philosophical thinking and in his later writings. He also frequently spoke about Intuition in lectures and addresses, sometimes briefly and on other occasions in detail and very instructively.

Over the course of time, the concept of Intuition underwent an interesting and significant transformation in Rudolf Steiner's work. Initially he chiefly spoke of it in connection with the sciences of organic nature, but subsequently it came to have a more profound and broader meaning as an essential source of supersensible knowledge. In combination with Imagination and Inspiration, Intuition furnishes the gateway through which supersensible knowledge is able to bring light into human knowledge.

Even the simplest thought is intuitive and possesses spiritual aspects. When thinking is schooled systematically it develops into an intuitive organ through which what is spiritual can be consciously comprehended and penetrated. Intuition links us to what is spiritually real and thus has an existential significance for our process of knowing.

When we consider the gradual evolution of Intuition through Anthroposophy we notice a conceptual development that shows us how alive and flexible anthroposophical concepts are in the way they develop and mature.

Rudolf Steiner clearly distinguishes between the spiritual

significance of the word Intuition and its everyday application. In general use it refers to a somewhat unclear or unfocussed impulse of feeling, whereas in Anthroposophy it denotes a clear, pure comprehension akin to a mathematical concept.

Intuition is the first supersensible form of knowledge to which Rudolf Steiner refers, namely in his introductory considerations regarding Goethe's scientific writings (in GA 1). Goethe's concept of Intuition takes us back to two thinkers: Kant and Spinoza.

Rudolf Steiner explains[1] how Goethe—as opposed to Kant—develops an intuitive science 'by means of observing ever-creative nature'. In the essay 'The Intuitive Power of Judgement', Goethe's starting point is Kant. According to Kant—and also according to Goethe—this is an understanding that is intuitive. Kant is thinking of an understanding which moves from an *intellectus archetypus*, 'from a synthetic generality, from a view of what is a wholeness as such', towards its separate parts, considering these and integrating them. Goethe develops this intuitive concept further both methodically and practically.

Steiner explains[2] how relevant Spinoza's conception of Intuition was for Goethe, and this enables him to describe his own way of thinking and method. For Spinoza, Intuition was the highest form of knowledge that exists. For Goethe, Intuition was the form of knowledge through which one can grasp what is alive, what is fundamental in organic nature. The spiritual archetype of the plant, the archetypal plant as such, is not visible as a wholeness; it develops over time in a living process of becoming. Intuition is what makes it possible to recognize the whole, the supra-temporal spiritual archetype, by means of the separate, sequential phenomena developed over time. In his later works Rudolf Steiner also describes the idea of the archetypal plant as an Intuition belonging to Goethe.

In his *Philosophy of Freedom* (GA 4), Steiner then links Intuition with the experience, through thinking, of essential being. The experience of thinking, the conscious perception and understanding of thinking, becomes an Intuitive thought process. Here, Intuition is a purely spiritual experience linking the human individual with the essence of reality through thinking.

In *Theosophy* (GA 9), Intuition is seen as having a central significance within the human individual. It links him with the world of spirit, just as the sensual organs reveal sense-perceptible reality for him. Intuitive thinking is a spiritual perceiving and as such it builds the bridge to the super-sensible world.

In *Stages of Higher Knowledge* (GA 12) and in *An Outline of Esoteric Science* (GA 13), Intuition appears together with the other two stages of supersensible knowledge: Imagination and Inspiration. Here we read of how, on the path of spiritual schooling, the human being ascends step by step from physical perception to Imagination, Inspiration and Intuition. Rudolf Steiner applies these three concepts in a specific and precise way. Imagination is supersensible seeing. Here supersensible knowledge appears in picture-form. Inspiration denotes the capacity to comprehend supersensible perceptions in meaningful connections with one another, just as, in reading, the individual letters of the alphabet are brought together to form words and sentences. That is why Inspiration is also described as 'reading the hidden script'. Intuition is the third and most elevated way of knowing, linking the human being with the very essence of reality. Intuition shows us the essence of the spirit, of the events in our life after death, and the spiritual process through which human beings and the world come into existence. Intuition enables us to investigate thoroughly the spiritual facts. There is no need necessarily to go through these three stages of spiritual knowledge in sequence, but it is one possible way of proceeding.

In Rudolf Steiner's later works, more is said about the three stages of supersensible consciousness, and here they are seen in the context of a variety of practical aspects. Especially in his spoken explanations about medicine, education, the natural sciences, the arts and social life, Intuition is depicted as one of the supersensible forms of knowledge in Anthroposophy which provide direct insight into practical life.

Occasionally in the earlier lectures the word Intuition is used in its everyday sense. For example 'intuitive' as an alternative to 'instinctual', 'unconscious' or 'of the feelings'; but these examples are infrequent. Steiner also occasionally uses adjectives such as 'instinctive Intuition', 'spiritual Intuition', 'obscure Intuition'. In such cases, 'Intuition' stands for 'higher seeing'—in other words, conscious spiritual perception. Only after 1909 is Intuition used frequently, and then very often in connection with Imagination and Inspiration.

In the present volume, Rudolf Steiner's *written* references to Intuition are the point of departure. Within each chapter these are arranged chronologically. Thereafter, important passages from the lectures are quoted with reference to different themes, and these, too, are arranged chronologically. The concept of Intuition is central to these quotations. Although these passages are not necessarily connected, they provide a representative and comprehensive overview regarding the genesis and development of the concept of Intuition within Anthroposophy.

One specific quotation calls for special explanation. In 1909, Rudolf Steiner depicted Intuition as a spiritual being. This is the only passage where Intuition speaks as a being of high rank, linked here with landscape painting, with Leonardo da Vinci's 'Last Supper', and with portrait painting.

In the final chapter, further aspects of Intuition are briefly presented in various practical contexts, for example in geometry, architecture, economics, education and medicine. This is of course merely a small selection that may serve as an encouragement toward further research.

This volume is intended as a contribution toward explaining the concept of Intuition as seen in Anthroposophy. By following a specific concept in its gradual transformation and amplification throughout the work of Rudolf Steiner, it also offers insights into how Anthroposophy evolved. The choice of the texts is intended to provide a stimulus for further research into the development of the term. It is hoped that awareness of how the concept of Intuition developed will help to encourage a living, meaningful link with the spiritual world.

Edward de Boer

1. The Perceptive Power of Judgement— Goethe's Intuition

So Goethe—in contrast to Kant—recognized that the human being has intuitive knowledge, which for him provided an explanation for what is organic. Goethe's organic 'type' is, I consider, very different from what today's Darwinism means by 'type'. It is the *unconscious* in the form in which it governs the organic world.

I think that with Goethe we have reached the turning point when what is organic is uplifted from being something unscientific to being a scientific method.[3]

Spinoza distinguishes between three forms of knowledge. The first is the way in which specific words we hear or read remind us of things in that we have specific conceptions of them resembling the way we represent them pictorially. The second type of knowledge is the way in which we form general concepts from our ideas of things. The third type of knowledge is the one through which we move forward from a perception of the true essence of some of God's attributes in order to arrive at an adequate knowledge of the true essence of things as such. This is the type of knowledge which Spinoza terms *scientia intuitiva*, knowledge *through perception*. This latter, the highest form of knowledge, is the one to which Goethe was aspiring. One must endeavour to understand what Spinoza meant by this: We must recognize things in a way that enables us to recognize in them some of God's attributes. Spinoza's God constitutes the world's content of ideas, that principle which sets everything in motion, which supports everything and which sustains all things. One may picture this either as an independent entity separate from all finite beings and existing side by side with them while controlling them and causing them to interact with one another. Or one may imagine this being as having become absorbed in the finite things so that it no longer exists above or beside them but is now solely within them. This view in no way denies the original principle; it recognizes it fully while regarding it as having *flowed out* into the world. The first view regards the finite world as a revelation of the infinite in such a way that this infinity remains within its own existence, without giving anything of itself away. It does not depart from itself, but rather remains as it was before becoming a revelation. The second view also regards the finite world as a revelation of the infinite, but it assumes that in becoming revealed it has departed entirely from itself and placed its own being and life into its creation, so that it now exists solely *within that*. However, since recognizing things involves becoming aware of the being of things, then, if the being can only exist as a part of the infinite, knowledge must be 'a becoming aware' of what is infinite in all things.[*4]

However, if we wish to recognize organic nature we must not regard the idea, the concept, as something that is an expression of something different, from which it borrows its content. We must rather recognize *the idea as such*. It is

---

[*] In other words, of some of God's attributes within the things.

necessary for it to possess its own content from within itself and not from the sense-perceptible world of space and time. This unit, which we conceive as something abstract, would have to be built upon itself, it would have to be constructed *out of itself*, out of its own being and not in accordance with influences from other objects. It would be impossible for the human being to understand such an entity that is formed out of itself and is revealed out of itself. What, then, is necessary for such a concept? A power of discernment that is able to confer upon a thought something which is taken in through something other than merely the external senses, something which is a pure idea independent of the sense-perceptible world. Such a concept, which is not derived from the sense-perceptible world but which has a content derived solely from itself and from the content that emanates from itself, may be described as an *intuitive concept*, and the knowledge derived from it is then intuitive knowledge. What follows from this is clear: *An organism can only be grasped by means of intuitive thinking.* Goethe showed through what he did that it is possible for the human being to have knowledge in this way.[5]

Once our mind has grasped the general idea, the type, it has comprehended the entire realm of the organisms in all its homogeneity. When it thus *observes* the formation of a type in each of its variations, the final one then becomes comprehensible as one of the stages, of the metamorphoses through which that type realizes itself. And demonstrating these stages would be the essence of the taxonomic system confirmed by Goethe. Both in the animal and in the plant kingdom there exists an ascending sequence of developments; organisms are classified as being either complete or incomplete. How can this be possible? The ideal form, the type of an organism, is characterized by elements belonging to both space and time. Goethe, too, saw this as a form which is both *sense-perceptible* and *supersensible*. It contains spatial and temporal forms as *intuitive* ideals. But when it appears in reality, that truly (no longer intuitively) sense-perceptible form either conforms entirely or does not conform entirely with the ideal. Lower organisms are what they are because the form in which they manifest does not entirely conform with their organic type. The more the external appearance and the organic type of a specific creature conform with one another, the more is that creature perfect. This is the objective foundation for an ascending developmental sequence. The analysis of this interrelationship within every organism has to be systematically depicted. But this cannot be included in listing the type and the primeval organisms; all that is possible is to find a form which would be the most perfect expression of that type. This is what Goethe's archetypal plant is intended to show.[6]

A way of thinking which shows a direct connection between content and form has always been described as *intuitive*.

Intuition as a scientific principle appears again and again. The English philosopher Reid said that Intuition is involved when the perception of external phenomena (sense impressions) leads to our conviction that they *exist*. Jacobi considered that our feeling for God represented the guarantee that God does exist. A judgement of this kind is also termed intuitive.[7]

Our power of judgement must *reflect in thinking* and *think in reflecting*. This, as Goethe was the first to point out, is the perceptive power of judgement. Herewith, Goethe indicated that *this* is what is necessary for understanding to come about in the human mind, whereas Kant wanted to have shown that this did not belong to the predisposition of the human being.

Whereas in organic nature the type represents the natural law (the archetypal phenomenon) of what is inorganic, so does Intuition (the perceptive power of judgement) provide proof through reflection.[8]

Frequently little value has been attached to Intuition in connection with science. Goethe's thinking was regarded as being defective owing to the fact that he wanted to reach scientific truths through Intuition. Many, however, consider Intuition to be very important in matters of scientific *discovery*. In this connection they say that a *brainwave* can frequently lead further than methodical thinking. People frequently speak of Intuition when someone arrives at a correct conclusion by chance and only subsequently realizes it to be true. But that Intuition in itself can be regarded as a scientific principle is always denied. When something has been discovered through Intuition, it must—so people think—be subsequently proven if it is to have any scientific value.[9]

The derogatory view of Intuition has more than a little to do with the way in which it is thought to be less credible than sciences that provide proof. Frequently, only what it has been possible to prove is described as being *knowledge*, whereas everything else is seen as being *belief*.

We must take into consideration that Intuition has an entirely different meaning within *our* scientific way of thinking, which gives us the conviction that through thinking we grasp the core of the world's being in its reality, whereas others regard this as taking it into a realm of the beyond which cannot be researched.[10]

For organic science, however, Intuition is the correct method. We regard our explanations as making it quite clear that Goethe's way of thinking, for the very reason that it was based on Intuition, had found the correct method with regard to the organic. The very method of the organic coincided with the constitution of his spirit.[11]

Our view of the world is not subject to the danger of having to consider that the limitations of a method of proof have to be regarded as the limitations of scientific conviction. It has shown us that the core of the world flows into our thinking, that we think not only *about* the nature of the world but that our thinking accompanies the essence of its reality. Intuition does not impose a truth upon us from outside because from our point of view *there is no such thing* as externality and internality of the kind supposed by the type of scientific thinking just described as being the opposite of our own. For us, Intuition is a direct way of being within, of penetrating into the truth which yields all that is there to be considered. It enters entirely into that which is given to us by our intuitive judgement. Utterly lacking here is the characteristic called for by *believing* that only the complete truth but not its reasons are given to us, so that we lack the penetrating view.

The insight gained through Intuition is just as *scientific* as whatever it has proven.[12]

If one wishes to arrive at the type, one is obliged to proceed from the individual form to the archetypal form; if one wishes to arrive at the spirit, one is obliged to disregard the expressions through which it makes itself known or the specific actions it accomplishes, and then to look at it on its own account. One has to listen to it and observe its actions, rather than how it behaves or has behaved in one situation or another. . . .

It is no longer, as was the case with organic things, that we observe the general form of something as its archetypal form; rather it is a matter of perceiving the specific as the archetype itself. The human spiritual being is not *one* manifestation of its idea but rather *the actual* manifestation of it. When Jacobi observes that through perceiving our own inwardness we are also gaining the conviction that it is founded on a uniform being (intuitive self-perception) then that is an error, because what we are perceiving is the individual being as such. What, otherwise, is Intuition is here observation of one's self. And this is objectively necessary with regard to the highest form of existence. What the spirit can gather from the manifestation, this is the highest form of the content obtainable. If it then reflects upon itself, it cannot help but recognize itself directly as the manifestation of that highest form, as the bearer of that same self. What the spirit discovers as a oneness within manifold reality, that is what it must find as the immediate existence of its own individuality. The generality as something specific is what it must present as its own individual being.[13]

If one recognizes thinking as a capacity for perception which goes beyond a comprehension through the senses, then one must also attribute to it the possibility of there being objects which lie beyond what is a merely sense-perceptible reality. *Ideas* are the objects of thinking. When thinking takes hold of ideas, it becomes fused with the primeval ground of world existence; that which is at work outside then enters into the spirit of the human being: it becomes *one* with objective reality at its strongest. *Becoming aware of the idea in reality is the true communion of the human being.*

With regard to ideas, thinking has the same significance as the eye has for light and the ear for sound. *It is an organ of comprehension.*[14]

The intuitive spirit is able to recognize the idea. But it can only perceive *individual* figures when it directs its senses outwards, when it observes and looks at things. The reason why a modification of the idea can only arise in this way, as a sense-perceptible reality, cannot be puzzled out; it has to be *sought* in the realm of reality.

This is Goethe's specific view, which might best be described as an *empirical theory*. It may be summarized in the words: Things which possess a *sense-perceptible multiplicity* are, insofar as they are homogeneous, founded upon a *spiritual uniformity* which brings about that homogeneity and that inter-connectedness.[15]

It is interesting to see how Schiller endeavours to explain the difference between Goethe's way of thinking and his own. He perceives the archetypal and independent freedom of

Goethe's world view. But he is unable to remove from his own thinking the one-sidedly Platonic elements of thought. He cannot reach the insight which tells that the idea and the perception are in reality not separate from one another but are only *thought* to be separate owing to an erroneous understanding. He therefore confronts Goethe's way of thinking, which he describes as being intuitive, with his own speculative way of thinking and thus claims that both, so long as they are sufficiently powerful, must lead to the same goal. Schiller assumes that the intuitive spirit holds to the empirical, individual way of thinking whence it then ascends to the legitimate idea. When such a thinker is a genius, then he will see the necessity in what is empirical and the species in what is individual. Of the speculative way of thinking Schiller assumes the opposite. It must begin with the law, the idea, and then descend to the empirical and individual. When a thinker of this kind is a genius he will still only pay attention to the species which, though, has the potential for life and a firm relationship with real objects. The assumption of a specific way of thinking, one that is speculative as opposed to intuitive, rests on the belief that the world of ideas must have a separate existence which is detached from the world of perception. If this were the case then it would be possible for the content of ideas to enter into the thinking via the content of perceptions even when this was not being sought for. However, if the world of ideas is inseparable from the reality of experience, then both exist as *a single* totality; and then only such intuitive knowledge could exist that seeks the idea through experience while also comprehending what is individual as being at one with the species. In reality there is actually no such thing as a purely speculative thinking in Schiller's sense. For the species exists solely within the sphere to which the individuals also belong; and thinking cannot find it anywhere else.[16]

There is at present much confusion regarding the concept of Intuition. We must realize that science today accepts the concept of Intuition only in the field of mathematics. Among today's sciences, Intuition is regarded as being solely a matter of inner perception. Yet such inner perception is not solely confined to figures applied to space, for it also refers to everything else. Goethe, for example, endeavoured to found an intuitive science also for the field of botany. In all its various metamorphoses, his 'archetypal plant' is founded upon an inner view.[17]

It was after a gathering of the Society for Scientific Research in 1794—presumably in July—that Goethe and Schiller, on their way home, entered into a conversation about the lecture they had just heard. Schiller said he found everything so disjointed, as though divided up into separate parts, whereupon Goethe said he thought it possible to imagine a different way of observing nature. He explained to him his view of there being an interrelationship among all living things, so that one should consider the entire plant world as being in continuous evolution. With a few strokes of the pen Goethe drew on a sheet of paper the archetypal plant he had discovered. 'But that is not a reality, it's an idea'—objected Schiller. 'Well, if it's an idea', said Goethe, 'then I can see my ideas with my own eyes.' This argument demonstrated the two men's way of thinking. Goethe saw the spirit in nature. What the spirit comprehends intuitively was for him just as real as what the senses perceive; for him, nature included spirit. Schiller's true greatness shows in the effort he made to fathom the basis of Goethe's thoughts. He wanted to find the correct point of view. In the way he accepted what he was being told without any envy, Schiller laid the foundation for the profound friendship which was to develop between the two men. After immersing himself in Goethe's endeavours, Schiller wrote a letter to Goethe on 23 August 1794 which is one of the most beautiful documentations of humanity. 'For a good deal of time, although from some distance, I have been observing the processes of your mind and noting with ever-growing admiration the path you have chosen for yourself. You have been seeking what is essential in nature, but you have been seeking it along the most difficult path which any weaker capability would most certainly avoid. You take nature as a whole in order to throw light upon the details: in the universality of its manifestations you seek the explanation for the individual parts.'[18]

Only the thought which is free from sense-perceptible content, which strives toward the character of eternity, which is viewed by the spirit when it no longer looks out through the gate of the senses but instead looks inward, only that thought amounts to the content of spirit. Western researchers know only such thought in a single realm, that of mathematics, geometry and algebra. Here there are thoughts which do not approach us from the external world but instead come to us from within, thoughts which we create intuitively. It would be impossible to arrive at a mathematical theorem solely on the basis of what we see. It would be impossible to ascertain, by merely looking, that the three corners of a triangle taken together amount to 180 degrees.

There are, however, thoughts which do not apply solely to space, pure thoughts which are sense-free and refer to everything else in the world, to minerals, plants, animals and indeed also to the human being. In his morphology, Goethe endeavoured to formulate a theory of plants which contains such sense-free thoughts. He wanted to fathom how nature lives in creativity. Someone who enters with feeling and empathy into what Goethe puts forward in his theory of metamorphosis will experience an immense elevation into etheric heights. If you allow yourself to be raised ever higher toward a comprehension of thoughts which are formed in emulation of spatial mathematics, then you will discover the great mystics who enlighten us about the soul and the spirit. That is why mystics call mysticism 'mathematics'—*Mathesis*—not because mysticism is mathematics but because it is constructed in accordance with the prototype of mathematics. Goethe was a mystic of this kind. He wanted to present us with a world which raises us up beyond the realm merely of soul into the realm of spirit. It brings us to what the human being can do with his mind in everyday life, this raising up of a reality which is immediately temporal and transitory to a higher level, the world of pure thinking. If you can rise up to pure thought, if you can abstract yourself from a thinking filled with sense-perceptions, then you will be able to experience within yourself something that belongs to eternity. Manas is the term in theosophy for this initial element of the spirit. In my book *Theosophy* I endeavoured to translate this as 'spirit-self'. It is the higher self which raises itself up beyond what is limited to the merely earthly world.[19]

We are rather inclined to state that mysticism is something unclear. But what is unclear is only the one who does not find his way to higher realms. In the pure heights of the etheric, mystics strive for the most precious clarity of concepts unimpeded by the brutality of immediate reality. Initially we need to take possession of the concepts which can lead us into that land of clarity. Goethe was searching for that land of clarity; he was striving for mathematical knowledge. Fifteen years ago I found among Goethe's effects an exercise book which confirmed that even into his latter years he was concerning himself with mathematical studies, or indeed with the most advanced questions. In keeping with the attitude of a genuine gnostic he also pursued studies of nature and of the human soul. For example, his intuitive spirit also enabled him to behold the archetypal plant.[20]

When, at the height of his insight (1828), Goethe was looking back to this stage [of natural science around the time of his move to Weimar], what he said was: 'I would be inclined to describe this stage of insight as a comparative which strives to express its direction as a superlative not yet attained ... The fulfilment still lacking was the view of the two great driving forces of nature: the concept of *polarity* and of *intensification*, the former with regard to matter in its corporeal sense and the latter, by contrast, as it applies to what is spiritual. The former is in a constant state of attraction and rejection while the latter strives permanently upwards. However, since matter is never without spirit and since spirit can never exist nor be effective without matter, matter is also capable of intensification while spirit cannot avoid the urge to attract or repel.' It was with these conceptions that Goethe approached the animal, plant and mineral worlds in his endeavour, through the evident multiplicity of their sense perceptible manifestations, to comprehend their hidden spiritual unity. This is how he arrived at what he termed the 'archetypal plant' and the 'archetypal animal'. And behind these ideas there stood for him the active spiritual force of Intuition. His entire being strove to gain from his observations what in Theosophy is termed *tolerance*.[21]

More and more, through the sternest inner self-education, [Goethe] sought to develop this capacity within himself. He used numerous expressions to describe his form of self-education. Let us here quote just one of these, from his *Kampagne in Frankreich* (1792). 'With little awareness I allowed myself to live from day to day which, especially in recent years, had little ill-effect upon me. I possessed the characteristic of never thinking in advance about a person I was about to encounter or a place I was about to enter. I allowed such things to influence me without preparing myself in any way. The great advantage of this is that there is then no need to step back from some preconceived idea or to eliminate an arbitrarily fancied image and thus uncomfortably accept reality in its place.' He sought in this way to rise ever higher before having to make a distinction between the real and the unreal.[22]

Wisdom is not merely science, but it must have science within it. It is science that has entered into life where at any moment a decision and an action will become necessary. Someone who knows only the laws is a scientist. A wise person is someone who at every moment knows how to apply science and thus bring about a positive outcome. Wisdom is science that has become fertile. We must forget what it was that led to the laws which must permeate us so that they may become a power within us. From an exact observation of the plant Goethe proceeded to the idea of the archetypal plant. It is a figure arising out of spiritual Intuition, an image of a plant that might live within us, and in accordance with which countless plants might be created that do not yet exist but could become capable of sustaining life. In the wise individual the laws become able to extricate themselves from the single example and live in eternity.[23]

Schiller [in the letter mentioned on page 16] tells how Goethe gains his views not speculatively but through seeking a basis for them in the universality of the world's phenomena. All is contained within Goethe's Intuition, and there is little need for him to borrow from philosophy, for it is from him that philosophy could learn.

In Goethe's way of viewing the world, in the inner attitude out of which he has created his works, Schiller sees something that leads the human being most profoundly into the mysteries of existence.[24]

We are thus able to see how Goethe truly worked in all fields. We can see how everywhere his quest for knowledge of the natural laws was inspired by the poetic powers he had within him. Nothing is separate within his soul; there is interplay among all that is within him. No aspect is an obstacle for any other aspect. Thus Goethe offers us living proof that it is entirely wrong, indeed absurd, to believe that a lively quest within some intellectual branch of learning might present an obstacle for Intuition. Where both impulses are present in all their power and originality neither presents an obstacle for the other.[25]

A second characteristic of Goethe, one which renders him the most modern spirit of the fifth post-Atlantean age, is the way in which, within his soul, there lives a specific spiritual direction that leads him from an intuitive view of nature to art. One of the most interesting aspects in studying Goethe is to pursue the interconnection between his view of nature and his soul's artistic activities, his artistic creativity and imaginative powers. One arrives not at hundreds but at thousands of questions, living questions, not pedantic, theoretical questions, when one considers his entirely individual, remarkable path that comes about in him when he studies nature artistically, though not at all unrealistically, and when he senses in art, as he said himself, something that is a continuation of divine natural creativity on a higher level.[26]

It is known in the widest circles that Goethe was not only active artistically but that he also gained insights—unfortunately one can nowadays not use the definition scientific as such—of a scientific kind into the weaving and living of all nature's processes and conditions. We need only remember how Goethe reached an understanding of how every separate part of a plant is a transformation of all the other parts present in that specific entity; of how one member of a being in nature is a metamorphosis of another member and indeed of the plant as a whole; and of how he applied this to higher organic entities as well, animals and the human being, so that the entity as an overall metamorphosis presents a compilation of all its main members. This was the conclusion reached by Goethe.

In imbuing oneself with the Intuition inherent in this view of nature, one becomes able to transpose such an insight into an artistic feeling and an artistic form. This is the endeavour undertaken here in our art of eurythmy through certain artistic movements of the human body itself. It is to be attained through translating what Goethe saw, initially in the form, into an artistically transformed movement.[27]

Nature does give us, in certain examples ..., the most wonderful insights if only we have the Intuition to seek for them in the appropriate aspects of nature.[28]

2. Moral Intuition—Experiencing Thinking

When we contemplate thinking as such, two aspects coincide which otherwise *must* always appear apart, namely concept and percept. If we fail to see this, we shall be unable to regard the concepts which we have elaborated with respect to percepts as anything but shadowy copies of those percepts, and we shall take the percepts as presenting to us the true reality. We shall, moreover, build up for ourselves a metaphysical world after the pattern of the perceived world; we shall call this a world of atoms, a world of will, a world of unconscious spirit, or whatever, each of us according to our own kind of mental imagery. And we shall fail to notice that all the time we have been doing nothing other than building up a metaphysical world hypothetically, after the pattern of *our own* world of percepts. But if we recognize what is present in thinking, we shall realize that in the percept we have only one part of the reality and that the other part, which belongs to it, and which first allows the full reality to appear, is *experienced* by us in a permeation of the percept by thinking. We shall see in this element that appears in our consciousness as thinking, not a shadowy copy of some reality, but a self-sustaining spiritual essence. And of this we shall be able to say that it is brought into consciousness for us through *Intuition*. Intuition is the conscious experience—in pure spirit—of a purely spiritual content. Only through an Intuition can the essence of thinking be grasped.[29]

The highest level of individual life is that of conceptual thinking without regard to any definite perceptual content. We determine the content of a concept through pure Intuition from out of the ideal sphere. Such a concept contains, at first, no reference to any definite percept. If we enter upon an act of will under the influence of a mental picture, then it is this percept which determines our action indirectly by way of the conceptual thinking. But if we act under the influence of Intuition, the driving force of our action is *pure thinking*. As it is the custom in philosophy to call the faculty of pure thinking 'reason', we may well be justified in giving the name of *practical reason* to the moral driving force characteristic of this level of life.[30]

For what is here effective as the driving force is no longer something merely individual in me, but the ideal and hence universal content of my Intuition. As soon as I see the justification for taking this content as the basis and starting point of an action, I enter upon the act of will irrespective of whether I have had the concept beforehand or whether it only enters my consciousness immediately before the action, that is, irrespective of whether it was already present as a disposition in me or not.[31]

While I am performing an action I am influenced by a moral maxim in so far as it can live in me intuitively; it is bound up with my *love* for the objective that I want to realize through my action. I ask no one and no rule, 'Shall I perform this action?'—but carry it out as soon as I have grasped the idea of it. This alone makes it *my* action.[32]

I acknowledge no external principle of my action, because I have found in myself the ground for my action, namely my love of the action. I do not work out mentally whether my action is good or bad; I carry it out because I *love* it. My action will be 'good' if my Intuition, steeped in love, finds its right place within the intuitively experienceable world continuum; it will be 'bad' if this is not the case. Again, I do not ask myself, 'How would another person act in my position?'. I simply act as I, a specific individuality, consider this to be what I should do. No general usage, no common custom, no maxim applying to all people, no moral standard is my immediate guide, except my love for the deed. I feel no compulsion, neither the compulsion of nature which guides me by my instinct nor the compulsion of the moral commandments, but I want simply to carry out what lies within me.[33]

I differ from my fellow human being not at all because we are living in two entirely different spiritual worlds but because from the world of ideas common to us both we receive different Intuitions. He wants to live out *his* Intuition, I *mine*. If we both really conceive out of the idea and do not obey any external impulses (physical or spiritual), then we cannot but meet one another in like striving, in common intent. A moral misunderstanding, a clash, is impossible between people who are morally *free*. Only the morally unfree, who follow their natural instincts or the accepted commands of duty, come into conflict with their neighbours if these do not obey the same instincts and the same commands as themselves. To *live* in love towards our actions and to *let live* in the understanding of the other person's will is the fundamental maxim of *free human beings*. They know no other *obligation* than what their will puts itself in unison with intuitively; how they will direct their *will* in a particular case their faculty for ideas will decide.

Were the ability to get on with one another not a basic part of human nature, no external laws could be able to implant it in us. It is only because human individuals *are* one in spirit that they can live out their lives side by side. The free person lives in confidence that he and any other free individuals belong to one spiritual world, and that their intentions will harmonize. The free individual does not demand agreement from his fellow human beings but expects to find it because it is inherent in human nature.[34]

A *free spirit* acts according to his impulses, that is, according to Intuitions selected from the totality of his world of ideas by thinking. For an *unfree spirit*, the reason why he singles out a particular Intuition from his world of ideas in order to make it the basis of an action lies in the world of percepts given to him, that is, in his past experiences. He recalls, before coming to a decision, what someone else has done or recommended as suitable in a comparable case, or what God has commanded to be done in such a case, and so on, and he acts accordingly. For a free spirit these prior conditions are not the only impulses to action. He makes a completely *firsthand* decision. What others have done in such a case worries him as little as what they have decreed. Purely ideal reasons lead him to select from the sum of his concepts just one in particular and then to translate it into action.[35]

Ethical behaviour is not based upon the eradication of all striving for pleasure to the end that bloodless abstract ideas may establish their dominion unopposed by any strong yearnings for the enjoyment of life, but rather upon a *strong will* sustained by ideal Intuitions, a will that reaches its goal even though the path be thorny.

Moral ideals spring from the moral Imagination of the human being. Their realization depends on his desire for them being intense enough to overcome pain and misery. They are *his* Intuitions, the driving forces which his spirit harnesses; he *wants* them, because their realization is his highest pleasure. He needs no ethics to forbid him to strive for pleasure and then to tell him what he *shall* strive for. He will strive for moral ideals if his moral Imagination is sufficiently active to provide him with Intuitions that give his will the strength to make its way against all the obstacles inherent in his constitution, including the pain that is necessarily involved.

If a person strives for sublimely great ideals, it is because they are the content of his own being, and their realization will bring him a joy compared to which the pleasure that a limited outlook gets from the gratification of commonplace desires is a mere triviality. Idealists *revel*, spiritually, in the translation of their ideals into reality.[36]

In the second part of this book [*The Philosophy of Freedom*] the attempt has been made to demonstrate that freedom is to be found in the reality of human action. For this purpose, it was necessary to single out from the whole sphere of human conduct those actions in which, on the basis of unprejudiced self-observation, one can speak of freedom. These are actions that represent the realization of ideal Intuitions. No other actions will be called free by an unprejudiced observer. Yet just by observing himself in an unprejudiced way, the individual will have to see that it is in his nature to progress along the road towards ethical Intuitions and their realization. But *this* unprejudiced observation of the ethical nature of the human being cannot, by itself, arrive at a final conclusion about freedom. For were intuitive thinking to originate in anything other than itself, were its essence not self-sustaining, then the consciousness of freedom that flows from morality would prove to be a mere illusion. But the second part of this book finds its natural support in the first part. This presents intuitive thinking as one's inwardly experienced spiritual activity. To understand *this* nature of thinking by *experiencing* it amounts to a knowledge of the *freedom* of intuitive thinking. And once we know that this thinking is free, we can also see to what regions of the will freedom may be ascribed. We shall regard the individual as a *free* agent if, on the basis of inner experience, we may attribute a self-sustaining essence to the life of intuitive thinking. Whoever cannot do this will never be able to discover a path to the acceptance of freedom that cannot be challenged in any way. This experience, to which we have attached such importance, discovers intuitive thinking *within consciousness*, although the reality of this thinking is not confined to consciousness. And with this it discovers freedom as the distinguishing feature of all actions proceeding from the Intuitions of consciousness.[37]

The argument of this book [*The Philosophy of Freedom*] is built upon intuitive thinking which may be experienced in a purely spiritual way and through which, in the act of knowing, every percept is placed in the world of reality. This book aims at presenting no more than can be surveyed through the experience of intuitive thinking. But we must also emphasize what kind of thought formation this experience of thinking demands. It demands that we shall not deny that intuitive thinking is a self-sustaining experience within the process of knowledge. It demands that we acknowledge that this thinking, in conjunction with the percept, is able to experience reality instead of having to seek it in an inferred world lying beyond experience, compared to which the activity of human thinking would be something purely subjective.

Thus, thinking is characterized as that factor through which the individual works his way spiritually into reality. (And, actually, no one should confuse this world conception, that is based on the direct experience of thinking, with mere rationalism.) On the other hand, it should be evident from the whole spirit of this argument that for human knowledge the perceptual element only becomes a guarantee of reality when it is taken hold of in thinking. *Outside* thinking there is nothing to characterize reality for what it is. Hence we must not imagine that the kind of reality guaranteed by sense perception is the only one. Whatever comes to us by way of percept is something that, on our journey through life, we simply have to *await*. The only question is: Would it be right to *expect*, from the point of view which this purely intuitively experienced thinking gives us, that the human being could *perceive* spiritual things as well as those perceived with the senses? It would be right to expect this. For although, *on the one hand,* intuitively experienced thinking is an active process taking place in the human spirit, *on the other hand,* it is also a spiritual percept grasped without a physical sense organ. It is a percept in which the perceiver is himself active, and a self-activity which is at the same time perceived. An intuitively experienced thinking individual is carried into a spiritual world also as perceiver. Within this spiritual world, whatever confronts him as percept, in the same way that the spiritual world of his own thinking does, will be recognized by him as a world of spiritual perception. *This* world of spiritual perception could be seen as having the same relationship to thinking that the world of sense perception has on the side of the senses. Once experienced, the world of spiritual perception cannot appear to the individual as something foreign to him, because in his intuitive thinking he already has an experience that is purely spiritual in character. Such a world of spiritual perception is discussed in a number of writings which I have published since this book first appeared. *The Philosophy of Freedom* forms the philosophical foundation for these later writings. For it tries to show that the experience of thinking, when rightly understood, *is* in fact an experience of spirit. Therefore it appears to the author that no one who can in all seriousness adopt the point of view of *The Philosophy of Freedom* will stop short before entering the world of spiritual perception. It is certainly not possible to deduce what is described in the author's later books by logical inference from the contents of this one. But a living comprehension of what is meant in this book by intuitive thinking will lead quite naturally to a living entry into the world of spiritual perception.[38]

We become familiar with our worldly *environment* through *observation*. Through *thinking* we penetrate into its very centre. Immersion within our own inner being solves the riddles of existence for us. The thought which lights up within me concerns not only myself but also the things it clarifies for me. My soul is simply the arena in which the things give expression to themselves.

However, in order to understand this the individual needs to have a living element in his thinking, something which is for him just as real, just as factual as are the things a less developed person encounters and can grasp with his hands. Someone who can only conceive of things that are copies of what he experiences through his senses cannot understand what is meant by thinking. In order to advance towards the essence of things, thinking must become filled with content which is not derived from the outer senses but from what flows out of the spirit itself. Thinking must be productive, intuitive. If it refrains from floating off into phantasy but instead resides in the light-filled clarity of inner vision, then what lives and weaves in it is the law of the universe itself. Of a way of thinking such as this, one may well say: The universe thinks itself in the thoughts of human beings. For this to come about it is necessary for the human individual to experience the eternal laws which thinking as such makes for itself. What people normally mean by 'thinking' is nothing but a muddled whirl of ideas.[39]

One may view the activity of thinking with the eyes of one's spirit. One may, for example, place a thought into the very centre of one's awareness where it refers to nothing external but is a symbol which one does not relate to anything external. And one may then persist in keeping a hold of such a thought. While thus persisting one may enter in a living way into the inner activity of the soul. This is not a matter of living in thought but of experiencing the activity of thinking as such. In doing this, the soul breaks loose from what it does in its normal thinking. If it persists long enough with such an inner exercise it will, after a while, recognize that it is entering into experiences which are separate from the thinking and reflecting that is bound up with the bodily organs. The same can be undertaken with regard to the feeling and willing of the soul, or indeed with the experiencing or perceiving of external things. In this manner one will only achieve something if one does not shrink from admitting that self-knowledge of the soul cannot simply be attained by looking inwards to what is always present; what is necessary is to seek what can only be revealed through *working* inwardly with the soul. Working with the soul in such a way that it leads to an entry into the inner activity of thinking, feeling and willing, such exercises bring about a kind of spiritual 'condensation' of those experiences. In this 'condensation' they then reveal their inner reality which cannot be perceived through normal consciousness. In working with the soul in this way one discovers that for ordinary consciousness to come about, the forces of the soul have to be diluted to such an extent that they become imperceptible. This form of working with the soul involves an *unlimited intensification* of capacities of soul which are also known to ordinary consciousness but which cannot be applied in this degree of intensification. These are the capacities of *attentiveness* and of *loving devotion to what the soul experiences.* In order to achieve what is meant here, these capacities must be intensified to a degree that enables them to work like entirely new powers of soul.[40]

Truth that is to be fruitful will always be a matter of searching and it will always have to 'falsify' what the fanatical fact-seeker wants. It resides infinitely far above this in that it creates something intuitive, something spiritual in the human being, adding something new to nature which would not exist without the human spirit. In this way, that which the human being cherishes in his dreams and creates in his spirit maintains more than what is significant as a mere luxury; it maintains cosmic truth in life as something which the human being has newly created. Thus, on the foundation of science, he ascends to productive work which flows freely from his soul as a primary Intuition. Following on from the highest stage of development he has a task that no other being in the world has, something that he adds which without him would not exist in all eternity.

Horrifying though such a view may be for someone interested solely in natural science, I regard as a true perception the fact that the human being has a right to be productive in his view of the world. This is a feeling that was alive in many ages before the fanaticism of facts and the theory of knowledge inflicted blinkers on us, ages during which conviction regarding the cosmic character of the world prevailed.[41]

What is required by a thought is that it should be permitted to become a reality.

A thought must be formed in a living way, just as is the case with the seed of a plant. Seeds can be sown, harvested and then used as food. This removes them from their proper path, which would involve the emergence of new plants from those seeds. Human beings have gathered the seeds of thought in this way, in the granaries of science and philosophy, where they have piled them up and left them to shrivel. In keeping with its nature, the seed of a plant must be immersed in an environment which brings it to life if it is to bud once again. Thus Hegel's thought-seeds need to be planted in the soil of spiritual science where they can grow up into a fruitful life, into the spiritual capacities of Imagination, Inspiration and Intuition. In place of the categorical imperative, the ego will activate a 'moral Imagination' out of the power of awakened thinking. When this happens it will also be possible to comprehend the approaching Christ-Impulse out of the forces of the earth. Through the paths pointed out by spiritual science, this is the connection between the world of thoughts in *The Philosophy of Freedom* and the higher powers of knowing coming into being in our soul.[42]

What I had written down [in *The Philosophy of Freedom*] was initially an ethical individualism. What I wanted to show in that way was that the human being would never be able to become free if his actions did not arise out of those ideas which are rooted in the Intuitions of the single human individuality. So that this ethical individualism, as the ultimate developmental goal of the human individual, would recognize the so-called free spirit which is working its way both out of the constraint of nature's laws as well as out of the constraint of all conventional so-called moral laws founded on trust; so that, in the age when evil approaches the individual's inclinations in the manner I described yesterday: then he may rise to Intuitions in order to transform those evil inclinations into what is good for the consciousness soul, what is genuinely worthy of the human being.[43]

Only that true human being is free who is regarded as an equipoise between the idea, which penetrates through to genuine spirit, and external, material reality.

Thus, in the book *The Philosophy of Freedom*, the endeavour was made not to found the moral life merely upon some abstract principle or other but upon the inner, moral experience which I at the time termed 'moral imagination'; upon that which in the individual human being as such, expressed pictorially, draws on Intuition. Kant put forward the categorical imperative: act in such a way that the maxims of your action can be a guiding principle for all human beings; clothe yourself in a jacket that fits all! The maxim of the freedom philosophy reads: act in a way which the spirit convinces you is right in the actual moment, in your individually concrete moment.

In this way, via the detour of moral philosophy, one enters into the spirit. Surely that could be the path along which present-day humanity might reach a view of the spiritual world: namely, if this humanity were to reach the not-all-too-difficult conclusion that morality lacks any steadfastness unless it is seen as being a part of what is supersensible and spiritual.[44]

The fact is noted by Professor Traub that in *The Philosophy of Freedom* I speak about intuitive thinking, but he has no idea what is meant by intuitive thinking. For him thinking is merely a formality and therefore merely vacuous. There is nothing one can discuss with such a person because he has failed to comprehend even the simplest of concepts such as those, for example, which in mathematics one acquires at the outset. For if thinking in mathematics were merely a formality without any content, I should like to know how one might reach any understanding of something like the Pythagorean theorem. If one wanted to base all content on experience one would never reach an understanding of the Pythagorean theorem, for that theorem presupposes that external sensual experience needs to be met with a thinking based on content, an intuitive thinking such as that described in *The Philosophy of Freedom*. That thinking of this kind has been developed is a fact of it having risen up as far as the spiritual world, and this is what must be emphasized when my *Philosophy [of Freedom]* is being described.[45]

When an individual advances towards developing an inner life within himself, so that he becomes able to frame the moral impulses for his actions in pure thoughts, then he becomes capable of basing his actions on genuine impulses of thinking and not merely on instinctive emotions, impulses of thinking that become immersed in external reality just as the one who loves becomes immersed in the beloved. That is when the human being is coming closer to his freedom. Freedom is as much a child of the thoughts formed in spiritual clear-sightedness—when there is no external compulsion—as it is a child of truly devoted love, the love for the purpose of the action. What German cultural life was striving for through Schiller when he stood up in opposition to Kant and felt an inkling of a similar concept of freedom, this is what it is appropriate for us to develop further in the present time. It has become clear to me that when considering what lies at the foundation of moral actions—even when people remain unaware of it, it is nevertheless present—one must describe this as Intuition. And that is why in *The Philosophy of Freedom* I spoke about moral Intuition.[46]

When an individual aspires to moral impulses through moral Intuition, thus becoming a genuinely free being, then he is—if I may be permitted to use that rather disliked word—already 'clairvoyant' with regard to his moral intentions. The impulses for all that is moral lie in whatever is above the sense-perceptible. Strictly speaking, truly moral rules are an outcome of human clairvoyance. Hence a direct path has arisen leading from my book *The Philosophy of Freedom* to what I now speak of as spiritual science. Freedom arises in a human individual solely when that individual develops himself. And he can also continue with his development so that when what he does is already founded on freedom it leads on to his becoming independent of all that is sense-perceptible and thus to his freely rising up into spiritual realms.[47]

Our moral life can only have any reality when spiritual vision impregnates and permeates all that we have gained over the course of three or four centuries. My intention is not to be critical in a reactionary way but simply to emphasize what is necessary. But what is it that our spiritual vision shows us, what is the moral element of our spiritual vision? This spiritual vision recognizes external nature, it sees the initial element of what rational geologists—comparatively speaking—presume to be the geological formation of the earth. Such geologists say that a great part of our earth's development is already proceeding along a downward path. In many regions of the world we are stepping on existence that is dead when we walk upon the land. This dead existence, however, is far more universal than what is merely geological; it also covers our cultural life, and in more recent times we have reached a science that focusses solely upon what is dead, what is lifeless, because in our cultural life we are surrounded by so much that is dying. We are becoming acquainted with that which is dying, with that which originated in the far distant past of evolution and has now reached its final phase in the earth's evolution. So we can compare what is now in its final phase with what is beginning to blossom within us in our moral ideals and Intuitions. What are these moral ideals and Intuitions? These moral ideals and Intuitions are revealing themselves to what we here refer to as anthroposophically-oriented spiritual science in such a way that we can see in them something which is comparable to the seed of a new plant, something which is contained in the blossom of a plant of which the legacy resides in the fading former blossom. We see how our moral life is budding within us. In experiencing what goes on in nature we experience what has developed in the earth out of former ages. In sensing how moral ideals begin to flourish, we experience how the earth, having been discarded as a corpse, will emerge with human souls into a cosmic, immortal life, just as the individual human being, when he discards his corpse, enters into an existence of spirit and soul. Thus, in developing our moral life, we see within ourselves the sprouting seeds of future earthly metamorphoses.[48]

That is why I endeavoured in my *Philosophy of Freedom* to point out that on the one hand the human being should not be aware solely of what he observes in nature through the ideas and conceptions passed on to him by modern natural science; for he can also develop this source within himself. And when he has comprehended that this source of inner soul life does not come from outside through observations made through his senses but that it comes from the soul itself, then he is educating himself to arrive at free decisions, to freely employ his will, and to act out of freedom. In *The Philosophy of Freedom* I endeavoured to show that one remains forever dependent if one follows only natural impulses; I endeavoured to show that one can only become free once one is capable of following one's own intuitive thinking, that intuitive, pure thinking which develops in the human soul itself. This indication concerning what the human being must himself educate within his soul if he is to become truly free, this indication made it necessary to develop further what I had hinted at in *The Philosophy of Freedom*, and I have endeavoured during recent decades to do this through what I have called anthroposophically-oriented spiritual science. Having indicated that the human being must himself bring forth from the depths of his soul the impulse for freedom, namely intuitive thinking, one must then further point out what results when the individual turns toward this inner source of his life of soul. Basically all my anthroposophical writings of subsequent years amount to what I indicated in my *Philosophy of Freedom*. What I have pointed out is that in one's soul there are paths to be followed in spirit which lead to a thinking that does not merely draw conclusions intellectually from one's surroundings but that, out of an inner vision, rises up to an experience of the spirit. I have been obliged to show what one sees when one looks into the spiritual world.[49]

An improvement can only be achieved by striving to attain for humanity what will gradually enable people to live with one another in a social way, filled to the brim with mutual trust. We must come to believe in human beings; we must come to believe that through a genuinely focussed education, through the development of our humanity, it may become possible, in the way we live, for us to get on with one another in our lives not merely as we do when we happen to pass one another in the street but in ways that involve actually meeting one another in the street. For when individuals meet one another in the street one of them passes on the left and the other on the right; they pass each other without bumping into one another. This is entirely a matter of course. If it becomes possible for the source of humanity, which I described in my *Philosophy of Freedom* as true Intuition, to open up, then it will be possible also in loftier matters of life to bring about a form of social community on a basis of trust similar to that of everyday life. After all, if two people meet on the street it is not necessary for a policeman to come and say: You should go this way so as not to bump into the other people. This matter of course in everyday encounters can also be introduced at higher levels of life where the seriousness of life exists, where the seriousness of life is cultivated.[50]

Once again we must find the bridge between the observation of nature and the observation of the spiritual world, not the generally vague spiritual world but that spiritual world which is the source of our moral Intuitions. I was already endeavouring to describe the interplay between the world of perceptions and the world of Intuitions in my *Philosophy of Freedom* in 1893. I wanted to show how the concrete moral Intuitions of a world which lies beyond the world of ordinary perceptions can be taken from there and inserted into this world.[51]

However, in that which we include in what is rhythmical, in what we pour, for example, into poetry, into pictures or indeed into anything cultural that lives in rhythms, and in what we include intuitively in our moral ideals, it is in this that we create something which survives earthly death, just as the individual human soul survives human death. The earth will perish in accordance with the laws of nature known to us today; in accordance with these laws the earth will perish. And in accordance with these laws, with which we are familiar, when we form moral Intuitions, when we form genuinely religious Intuitions in accordance with these laws, human souls will depart from the earth when it falls into death, and will move on into a future existence.[52]

3. The Human Being—Intuition as a Bridge to the Spirit

The spirit-self is a revelation of the spiritual world within the I, just as from the other side sense perceptions are a revelation of the physical world within the I. In whatever is red, green, light, dark, hard, soft, warm, cold we recognize the revelations of the bodily world; and in what is true and good we have the revelations of the spiritual world. Similarly, just as the revelation of what is bodily is termed sensation, so is the revelation of what is spiritual termed Intuition. Even the simplest thought contains Intuition, for it can neither be touched by the hands nor seen by the eyes—its revelation must be received from the spirit by the I.[53]

The I of the human being as it lives in the soul reaches out for messages from above through Intuition, and similarly it reaches out for messages from the physical world through sensations. It thus causes the spiritual world to be its inner life of soul just as the physical world is the inner life of the senses. The soul, or indeed the I which lights up within it, opens its portals in two directions: on the one hand towards what is bodily and on the other towards what is spiritual.[54]

In order to comprehend the entire human being one has to think of him as being composed of the parts described. The body is constructed from the physical world of substance in a way which orients it towards the thinking I. It is permeated by life forces and thus becomes the etheric body or life-body. As such it opens itself outwards through the sense organs and becomes the soul-body. The sentient soul permeates this and becomes one with it. The sentient soul not only receives impressions of the external world as sensations; it also has its own life which, on the other hand, is stimulated just as much through thinking as it is through sensations. Thus it becomes the intellectual or mind-soul. This it makes possible through opening itself upwards towards Intuitions in the same degree as it does downwards through sensations. So then it is the consciousness soul. This is made possible because the world of spirit forms within it the organ of Intuition just as its physical body forms in it the organs of sense. Just as the senses give it sensations through the soul-body, so does the spirit give it Intuitions through the organ of Intuition.[55]

True Intuition is received neither through logical thinking nor through conjectural thinking. Rather, the spirit of the individual is confronted directly by a truth. He *is sure* of it and needs no convincing.[56]

Just as ... the human being rises up to create images and Intuitions, so, before his existence, did the external world work in such a way that in everything that is mineral around us, in whatever is purely physical in nature, Intuitions work as creative forces. A crystal is external in the way it presents itself to the senses; but is was created through Intuitions. Behind the entire physical world there lies a cosmos of Intuitions and, ultimately, a being, the spirit of the planet, who brings forth those Intuitions.[57]

All that is intuitive in human beings, the great impulses they receive from the loftiest initiates, these are actually what overcomes the karma of facts. The one who rises to true Intuitions is penetrating through the physical world right up to the father spirit. The one who perceives intuitively can influence actual karma. He begins consciously to restrict his karma.

To an ordinary individual only those beings appear comprehensible who are themselves conscious. If he attains Imagination, then he can comprehend life; and when he attains Intuition he can press forward right up to the intuitive powers.[58]

The future is forever coming towards us. If life were to move only in one direction, nothing new would ever arise. The human being possesses genius—that is his future, his Intuitions, which are flowing towards him.[59]

We have frequently spoken about this builder of the human body in lectures on spiritual science. We have said that what is called the ether-body, a subtle body, underlies the physical body in all its matter, its substances and fluids, and that this ether- or life-body contains forces which build up the physical body. In fact, every organ is built up out of this ether-body. In order to study this ether-body one needs not only physical research but also something else as well, namely what one calls Intuition, spiritual research.[60]

And when this intuitive sense flows inwards, then there arises what we now call thinking, the forming of thoughts. This is what arises when the activity of the intuitive sense flows inwards.[61]

Primarily, the sentient soul will gradually be eliminated when the astral body itself is finally overcome through our making the interests of the world our own and through thus progressing more and more beyond our personal feelings. This results in the sentient soul, all inner impulses, inner passions and emotions being transformed into Intuitions. The sentient soul will then be replaced by the Intuition-soul. Thus we can now ... describe an individual with well-developed occult powers by saying: Although he also consists of an astral body, an etheric body and a physical body, he inwardly also consists of the Intuition-soul, the Inspiration-soul and the Imagination-soul, and this then leads him on to the spirit self.[62]

So it might be that an individual only develops as far as the sentient soul, which means that he allows himself to be governed entirely by his personal lusts, urges and so on. If such an individual were to be twisted upwards by occult means, the consequence would be that his sentient soul would be transformed into his Intuition-soul so that he would indeed have certain Intuitions. But those Intuitions would be nothing but transformations of his own personal lusts, urges and instincts.[63]

In the present cycle of humanity the consciousness soul is located in the physical body, which means that it makes use of its physical implements. The intellectual or mind-soul in the etheric body means that it makes use of its etheric movements. The sentient soul, which contains urges, lusts and passions, makes use of the forces that are located in the astral body. The mind-soul which contains, for instance, the inner powers of feeling, makes use of the etheric body; the consciousness soul makes use of the physical body's brain.

If in this sense the sentient soul is transformed into the Intuition-soul, you will have to realize that the Intuition-soul has its tools in the human being's astral body. The Inspiration-soul is the transformed intellectual or mind-soul. Its tools are located in the human being's etheric body. And the Imagination-soul, the transformed consciousness soul, has its tools in the human being's physical body.... The Imagination-soul does indeed enter into the physical body, penetrating it in such a way that the clairvoyant consciousness, the more it finds itself facing a developed human being, finds the limbs of the physical body permeated by ever higher and higher Imaginations which are pressed down by the inner being of that personality into the physical body. In the ordinary individual a number of Imaginations are present which are imprinted into the members of his body by higher spiritual beings. In the more developed individual there are added to the Imaginations, already present in his physical body, those Imaginations which he himself imprints into the members of his body from out of his own inner being. Thus do the organs of the physical body of an individual trained in occult matters become ever more enriched.[64]

Intuition arises when the individual pre-eminently seeks his world view through what lights up in him intuitively....

Someone who searches for the best he can have in his soul through allowing his Intuitions to flourish within himself, such a one resembles, and can be compared with, the Intuitive poet whose inspired soul sings of the moon, of the silvery, gentle light of the moon. Just as one can link the light of the moon with visionary fantasy, so must one relate to the moon the Intuitive individual referred to here.[65]

In the activity of the will one's I is asleep. What is experienced in unconscious Intuitions is experienced in a sleeping consciousness. The human being is constantly experiencing unconscious Intuitions; but they live in his will. He is asleep in his will which is why in ordinary life he is unable to bring them up into consciousness. They come into life only in very fortunate moments, and then the individual has only a very muted experience of the spiritual world.[66]

When one gains self-knowledge through Intuition, it turns out that the self-knowledge one has gained through Intuition is something incomplete; one only understands this when one realizes that on the other hand there is a situation which is similarly reversed from that of the sense organs. The senses are, as it were, inlets into which the external world projects with its laws. On the other hand, where the entire human being has become a sense-organ through Intuition, he is the one who projects into the spiritual world. Here the external world projects into the human being; there the human being projects into the spiritual world, or rather into the spiritual external world. Whereas up there . . . the human being has an active relationship with the dimension of depth, he initially gains a certain relationship with the dimension of height if, within his Intuition, he remains close to his self-knowledge.[67]

Something closely resembling sense-perception arises, only it is reversed. The human being in his entirety projects into the spiritual world through Intuition. Just as through his senses the external world projects into him, so does he through Intuition project consciously into the spiritual world. This conscious entry is felt by the human being in the same way as he feels the external world through perception. And this feeling of being within the spiritual world, this shadowy experience of being within the spiritual external world, is termed Intuition in ordinary life. This Intuition becomes permeated by bright clarity when the kind of knowledge I have been describing is striven for. From this you will gather that we have perception as the one aspect of the human being's relationship with the world outside him. And on the other hand we also have as perception something inde-terminate which must initially be worked on. Just as per-ceptions have to be worked on intellectually in order to discover laws within those perceptions, so is there also on the other hand something with which the human being has an equally indeterminate relationship as he has with percep-tions, something which has to be dealt with and penetrated—just as formerly the external perceptions had to be permeated with mathematical precision by means of the inner knowl-edge gained through ordinary experience.[68]

What one has initially in the ordinary experience of as yet indeterminate Intuition is an experience of belief, of faith. At the one extremity of the human being, when he turns towards the external world, he has an experience of perception; similarly, just as perception can be permeated by understanding and reason, so can that which lies within an indeterminate, shadowy experience of belief, of faith be illumined by ever increasing understanding. And then what was an experience of belief, of faith can become a scientific result just like a perception at the other end becomes a scientific result when it is worked through. This is how things are. What I am describing to you here is similarly an ascent involved in transforming an ordinary experience of belief, of faith, through inner spiritual work into an experience of knowledge and understanding. For an individual as he ascends into these regions through transforming an experience of belief, of faith into an experience of knowledge, the experience is the same as for someone presented with a perception who then proceeds to work on it with mathematical or any other logical means.[69]

When one has at last trained oneself in Intuition, when one no longer feels what one has learned in life to be mere walking, but when one feels oneself to be the other individual who is active and who exists, when one entirely permeates the other individual, then Intuition is reached. And then one comprehends the I and the will in such a way that one can say:

The etheric body is comprehended through
　Imagination,
the astral body is comprehended through Inspiration,
the I is comprehended through Intuition.

In everyday life one does not possess the I, for the I sleeps. One only knows of one's I, which is asleep, in the shadowy way in which one knows in the dark that it is dark. The objects that exist there are not obvious. Thus the I also sleeps.

By thinking very strenuously one can find what I described from the beginning in my book *Theosophy*: physical body, etheric body, astral body, I. And then one can also point out how the members of the human being can be comprehended visually through Imagination, Inspiration and Intuition.[70]

Thus one must picture to oneself the metabolic-limb system of the human being in such a way that the physical arms and so on are in reality spiritual and that in this spiritual element the I can develop. As I move my arms, my legs, secretions are constantly occurring, and these secretions can be seen. But they are not the essential element to which I am referring. If you want to explain to yourself what is there when the arm, the hand takes hold of an object, you must refer not to something physical but to something spiritual; the spiritual element which is there alongside the arm, that is what is important with regard to the human being. What you actually see is merely a secretion from the metabolic-limb system.

Indeed, how might one even embark on a karmic consideration if one believes that what one sees in the metabolic-limb system is a human being? It is no such thing. One can only embark on a karmic consideration when one knows what the human being actually is. And that which must be present in the consideration, although it is also present in the sense world, is an as yet supersensible image of Intuition.[71]

This is very interesting, for in considering the human being we have images for Intuition, Inspiration and Imagination. And in a thorough consideration of the metabolic-limb human being one can learn what Intuition really is in the supersensible.[72]

4. The Schooling Path—Spiritual Development and the Power of Intuition

In the section 'Philosophy', Dr. Rudolf Steiner lectured on 'Mathematics and Occultism'.[*] He considered that Plato required his pupils to have had prior training in mathematics, that the Gnostics termed their higher wisdom 'mathesis', and that the Pythagoreans regarded number and form as the basis of all existence. He explained that none of them were referring to abstract mathematics but that what they meant was the *intuitive view* of occultism which in the higher worlds comprehends laws with the help of a spiritual feeling that represents in the spiritual sense what music represents in our normal sensory world. Just as the air, through oscillations which may be expressed in numbers, brings about musical sensations, so can the occultist, when he prepares himself through a recognition of numerical secrets, perceive in the higher worlds a spiritual music which, in more highly developed individuals, can rise to a sensing of the music of the spheres. This music of the spheres is not an illusion; for an occultist it is a genuine experience. By incorporating mathesis into his own being, by permeating his astral and his mental body with the intimate meaning expressed by numerical relationships, the individual enables hidden world phenomena to work upon him.[73]

---

[*]Steiner is here reporting, in the third person, on the Theosophical Congress in Amsterdam.

Finally, at the *fourth stage of knowledge*, Inspiration also ceases. Of those elements usually recognized by every-day knowledge, only the I can still be taken into account. It is a specific inner experience which shows the mystery pupil that he has risen to this stage. This experience is expressed in the feeling that he is no longer *outside* the things and processes with which he is familiar but that he is now *within* them. Images are not the external reality; they simply *give expression* to it. Similarly, what Inspiration has to offer is also not the external reality, for it merely *gives expression* to it. What now, however, lives in the soul is the reality itself. The I has streamed across all beings; it has streamed into becoming at one with them. *Living* the things in the soul is now *Intuition*. Quite literally one can say of Intuition: through it one slips into all things. In ordinary life the individual possesses only *one* Intuition, and that is the Intuition of the I itself. For the I can in no way be perceived externally; it can be perceived solely within one's inner being.[74]

Every object in the external world can be given the same name by all individuals. A table can be called 'table' by everyone, a tulip can be called 'tulip' by everyone, and Herr Müller is addressed as 'Herr Müller' by everyone. But there is one word which an individual can only say of himself. That is the word 'I'. No one can address me as 'I', because for every other person I am 'you'. And in the same way every other person is 'you' for me. One can address only oneself as 'I'. This arises because one lives not *outside* but *inside* the I. And in a similar way one lives in all things through *intuitive* knowledge. Perception of one's own I is the prototype of all intuitive knowledge. However, in order to enter into things in this way one first has to step out of oneself. One has to become 'selfless' in order to fuse with the 'self', with the 'I' of another individual.[75]

Meditation and concentration are the sure means by which one can rise to this stage as also to the former stages. These have to be practised in a quiet and patient manner. It is a mistake to believe that one can rise up to the higher worlds tumultuously or by force. Such a belief would be entered into by someone expecting the reality of higher regions to approach him just as does that of the sense world. Full of life and rich though those regions may be to which one ascends, yet they are delicate and subtle, whereas the world of the senses is rough and rude. The most important lesson to learn is that one must become accustomed to describing something as being 'real' which is entirely different from what one describes as real within the sense-perceptible sphere. This is not easy. That is why frequently someone who wants to tread this mystery path is frightened away even as he takes the first steps. He expects things similar to tables and chairs to come towards him, but what he finds are 'spirits'. And because 'spirits' are not solid like tables and chairs they appear to him as 'something imagined'. This is simply because they are unfamiliar to him. It is necessary first of all to develop proper perception for the spiritual world, and then one will not merely view the spirit but also *recognize* it. A large part of mystery schooling involves this proper recognition and assessment of what is spiritual.[76]

Knowledge through Inspiration leads the individual to an experience of the *processes* of the invisible worlds, for example of the development of the human being or that of the earth and its planetary incarnations; but if within these higher worlds one is concerned not only with *processes* but also with *beings*, then *Intuition* must become the means to knowledge. What is brought about by such beings is recognized in images through Imagination, what is brought about by laws and conditions is recognized through Inspiration; and if one wishes to encounter the beings themselves, then Intuition is what is needed.[77]

The spiritual observer can rise from Inspiration to *Intuition*. This word as used in spiritual science signifies in many ways the exact opposite of something frequently experienced in ordinary life. In ordinary life we speak of intuition when looking at a vague idea which we feel to be true but which as yet lacks a clear conceptual description, something which represents an earlier stage of knowledge rather than knowledge itself. In accordance with this, such an 'idea' might light up in a flash as being a great truth; but it can only be valid as knowledge once it has been proven by means of conceptual judgements. We may describe as an Intuition something which we 'feel' to be true, something about which we are entirely convinced but which we do not want to burden by means of intellectual judgements. Some individuals who are approaching knowledge through spiritual science frequently say: This has always been 'intuitively' clear to me. All such matters must be put to one side when using the word 'Intuition' in the true sense we are discussing here. In the sense meant here, Intuition is not knowledge that is less clearly comprehended but rather knowledge that possesses a greatly superior degree of clarity.[78]

Experiences of the higher worlds express their significance in Inspiration. The observer is living in the characteristics and deeds of the beings of the higher worlds.... Even in Imaginative knowledge, for example, the observer experiences himself as living not outside but within the colour images; but he knows that these colour images are not independent beings but rather the characteristics of such beings. In Inspiration he realizes that he becomes one with the deeds of such beings, with the manifestations of their will. Not until he reaches Intuition does he merge with beings who are enclosed within themselves. This can only come about in the right way when this merging is not a matter of his becoming extinguished but when it involves the full preservation of his own being. Any 'becoming lost' within an extraneous being is wrong. Therefore only an I which is to a high degree firm within itself can merge with another being without being harmed. One has only grasped such a 'something' once one has attained the feeling: In this there is a being which is of the same kind and inner wholeness as my own I.[79]

Imagine seeing a person on the street. Initially the impression is fleeting. Later one becomes better acquainted; and then the moment arrives when the two souls open up to one another in friendship. When the veils fall from the souls so that one I encounters the other I, that is an experience which may be compared with what occurs when a stone appears to a spiritual observer as being merely an external manifestation from which he proceeds to something else that also belongs to the stone, just as a fingernail belongs to the human body; thus one experiences an 'I' that is living in the same way as one's own 'I' lives.

Not until he reaches Intuition does the individual experience the form of knowledge which takes him into the 'inner being' of things.[80]

A further stage of knowledge makes it possible to recognize these beings themselves in their own inner being. This stage of knowledge may be termed intuitive knowledge. (Intuition is a word that is misused in ordinary life to describe an unclear, indeterminate insight into something, a kind of idea which may be partly true but which cannot initially be proven. What is described here has of course nothing whatever to do with this type of 'Intuition'. What is meant with Intuition here is knowledge of the highest, most enlightened order of which, if one possesses it, one is aware in the fullest sense.) To recognize a sense-perceptible being involves being *outside* it and assessing it in accordance with the external impression it makes. To recognize a spiritual being through Intuition involves becoming entirely at one with it, becoming fully united inwardly with it. The pupil of the spirit rises to such knowledge step by step. Imagination enables him to feel that his impressions of a being are no longer those of its external manifestation but that they are rather a recognition of what flows from it in soul and spirit. Inspiration leads him further into its inner being: he learns through it how to understand what such beings mean for one another. In

Intuition he enters fully into those beings. What is meant by Intuition can be gleaned from what is described in this book [*An Outline of Esoteric Science*]. The foregoing chapters described not only the progress from the Saturn, Sun, and Moon developments, and so on, but also how beings participated in this progress in the most various of ways. The Thrones or Spirits of Will, of Wisdom, of Movement and so on were introduced. In connection with the development of the earth, the Spirits of Lucifer and of Ahriman were discussed. The building of the world was attributed to the beings involved. It is through intuitive knowledge that one can discover what is known about these beings.[81]

When supersensible knowledge has risen to Intuition it lives within a world of spiritual beings. These beings too undergo developments. Present-day humanity reaches, as it were, up as far as the world of Intuition. The human being also, of course, receives influences from even higher worlds during his development between death and a new birth; but he is not directly aware of these influences—the beings of the spiritual world bring them to him. And when we consider these beings we find everything they contribute to the human being. But as regards matters concerning them alone, and what they need for themselves in order to promote human evolution, this can only be ascertained through knowledge that reaches beyond Intuition.[82]

Meaningful decisions, for example, belong within the earthly realm to the very highest, while the effects of the mineral kingdom belong to the very lowest. In those higher realms, meaningful decisions belong approximately to what works as the mineral kingdom on earth, whereas the region in which the world plan is woven out of spiritual origins lies above the realm of Intuition.[83]

When the pupil of the spirit has reached an experience of Intuition he will know not only the images of the world of soul and spirit, he will be capable not only of reading the 'hidden script'; he will, indeed, reach an understanding of the beings themselves through whose collaboration the world to which human beings belong has come into existence. And he will thus also learn to recognize himself in the form which he possesses as a spiritual being in the world of soul and spirit. He will have worked his way through to a perception of his higher I, and he will have discovered how he must continue to work in order to gain control of his double, the 'Guardian of the Threshold'. But he will also have encountered the 'Greater Guardian of the Threshold' who stands before him as the one who constantly calls upon him to continue with his work. This 'Greater Guardian of the Threshold' now becomes the example he strives to follow. When this desire arises in the pupil of the spirit he will have reached the ability to recognize *who* exactly is standing before him as the 'Greater Guardian of the Threshold'. For now the pupil of the spirit perceives that this Guardian is transformed into the figure of Christ.... The pupil of the spirit is himself now initiated into the lofty mystery with which the name of Christ is united. The Christ reveals Himself to him as the 'great earthly human prototype'. Once the Christ has been recognized in this way through Intuition in the spiritual world, then it becomes possible to understand what took place historically on earth during the fourth post-Atlantean epoch of development (the Greco-Latin period). How the lofty Sun Being, the Christ Being, intervened in the earth's evolution and how this continues to work within the earth's evolution—this will become for the pupil of the spirit a perception he has himself experienced. Thus, through Intuition, the pupil of the spirit receives an explanation about the meaning and significance of the earth's evolution.[84]

The actual human being, the one who raises humans up above the animal world, is recognized through a mode of knowing which is even higher than Inspiration. Anthroposophy here speaks of Intuition. Inspiration reveals a world of spiritual beings; through Intuition the human individual with knowledge enters into a closer relationship with that world. One becomes fully aware of what is purely spiritual, something which, as conscious experience explains, has nothing whatever to do with what is experienced through the body. One thus enters into a life in which the human spirit lives among other spiritual beings. In Inspiration the spiritual beings *reveal* themselves to the world; through Intuition one *lives* with those beings.

Thus one comes to recognize the human being's fourth member, his actual I.[85]

If one wishes to find a fitting formulation for this condition of soul, one may say: Consciousness now experiences itself as an arena upon which supersensible content is not introduced but rather introduces itself. (In my book *Knowledge of the Higher Worlds* I termed this form of knowing 'intuitive

knowing', although one must beware of the ordinary sense of
the word 'intuition' which is used to characterize any feeling
content an experience might involve).

Direct soul-observation discovers that the whole relationship an individual has as a 'soul' with his physical body is
transformed through intuitive knowing. For spiritual insight
the etheric body as such reveals itself to be a differentiated
supersensible organism. And one recognizes that its differentiated members are associated with the limbs of the physical body in a specific way. One experiences the etheric body
to be the primary element and the physical body as its likeness, as something secondary.[86]

The type of meditative life described thus far* amounts to
supersensible self-awareness. But this would lack any
supersensible environment if this type of meditation were not

---

* 'It is solely a matter of strengthening self-awareness to the extent that one
can notice that something supersensible is revealed through perception.
And that which reveals itself, as the weakest initial announcement of an
experience of the soul in the supersensible realm, is able to continue
developing. It comes about when an individual creates, within his meditative life, a form of thinking which arises out of a combination of two
activities of soul, the one that lives through perceiving in ordinary consciousness and the one that works in ordinary thinking. In this way the
meditative life becomes a strengthened form of thinking, a thinking that
takes into itself the strength which otherwise flows out through perceiving.
Thinking must strengthen itself to the extent that it gains the same degree
of aliveness as that which is otherwise only present in perceiving. Without
sense-perception, thinking must work in a way that is not supported by
memory but instead gains its content in the immediate present, as is
otherwise only the case with perceiving.'

accompanied by another. To understand this other type one must turn one's attention to the activity of the will. In ordinary life the will is consciously directed towards external activities. But side by side with this there is also another expression of will in the human being to which very little attention is consciously paid. This is the expression which, during the course of life, guides the soul life of the human being from one stage of development to another. Not only is the individual every day filled with soul content different from that of the previous day; but on each subsequent day his soul-life also develops out of that of the previous day. And the driving force of this development is the will which, in this field of its activity, remains largely unconscious. However, through a developed observation of the self, this specific aspect of the will can be raised up to consciousness. And through this raising-up one becomes aware of a will which has nothing whatever to do with processes of a sense-perceptible world but which, independently of a sense-perceptible world, is directed towards an internal soul development. Once one has become familiar with this will, one gradually becomes accustomed to entering in the manner described above [in the footnote] into a meditative experience of soul activity that combines thinking and perceiving. And then this experience within the will-element expands to become an experience of a supersensible external world. The supersensible self-consciousness developed in the manner described experiences itself, through having been transferred into this will element, as existing within a supersensible environment filled with spiritual beings and processes. Whereas supersensible thinking leads to a self-awareness which does not use a memory faculty bound to the human organization of sense-perceptions, so does super-sensible will live in such a way that it becomes entirely filled with a spiritualized capacity for love. And this is what enables the human being's supersensible self-awareness to compre-hend perceptively the supersensible external world. The supersensible comprehension is brought about by a self-awareness which eliminates ordinary memory and which, through an Intuitive grasp of the spiritual external world, lives within a spiritualized power of love.

Only when one can comprehend the essence of this supersensible knowledge can one become capable of understanding what is meant by knowledge about nature. Knowledge about nature is essentially connected with the knowledge that develops in the human being within the physical, sense-perceptible world.[87]

In the inwardness of his soul, the mystic experiences the spirit directly in three members: firstly the Father spirit, Aristotle's unmoved mover; secondly the yearning in the soul for the unmoved mover: the Word or Logos; thirdly a coming alive in the spiritual world: this is the Spirit.

The soul can immerse itself within itself, can see spiritually, through Inspiration or Intuition. The mystic says: When I look out into nature, its force works upon me and I sense the force that is working upon me—the energy, the force of life. When the soul immerses itself in the outside world it must, according to Aristotle, become ensouled through feeling. He says: If I wish to see the unmoved mover, I must be free of all external sensations. This immersion of the soul he calls catharsis, purification. In accordance with catharsis, the soul unites with the spirit when it becomes intuitive, when it does not unite with the sensations from the external world.[88]

If a symbol affects the spirit of a human being in such a way that it releases intuitive powers, then that is a genuine symbol.[89]

The spiritual scientist receives an intuitive concept in an inner experience and is not obliged to go through any number of separate experiences. This is the same with someone who has seen, for example, a lion and can then create the concept 'lion'.

In the same way the spiritual scientist conceives of astral and mental beings as one through seeing them together. There are archetypal images for all spiritual things. Just as an artist can have an intuitive image in his head and then paint a hundred pictures in accordance with this image, so in the higher realms there are archetypal images for all things seen by the clairvoyant. Reading in the archetypal images of things, in the archetypal foundations, this is termed occultism. Reading in the ten-page book.[90]

The realization 'I am' can never be anything other than the human being's most intimate inner experience. Whatever it is that utters this sentence within the soul can only speak thus from within. And just as this seemingly empty *affirmation* of one's own self occurs, so do *all* higher occult experiences occur. They may become more filled with content and with life, but they all follow the same *pattern*. As Fichte described, one can encounter the type of all occult experiences initially entirely in the realm of thought. It is therefore correct to say that in saying 'I am' the god in the human individual begins to speak.[91]

Then we finally reach an even higher world that is opened up by even higher senses. The Rosicrucian method describes it as the world of true Intuition, whereby Intuition is something far more lofty than what is meant by the trivial application of the word in ordinary life; it is a blossoming, a stealing into the beings so that one comes to know them from within. In the movement that is affiliated with the Rosicrucians, this world of Intuition is termed the world of reason. This world is so far above the ordinary world that it casts only a vague shadow-image within the human world. The concepts of reason are feeble shadow-images in comparison with what are realities in that world.[92]

And then there is a yet higher stage of consciousness which we call Intuition in the true sense of that word, where the human being can steal right into things. This is not merely the consciousness of Inspiration. It is where the human being can, as it were, immerse himself in the beings and become identical with them.[93]

We have just said[*] that we must in a way tear out of our soul what we have previously gained and that by doing this we

---

[*] 'Whatever [a person] is most strongly tempted to believe in, whatever he loves the most, whatever would already constitute the greatest happiness for many, this is what the individual must tear out by its roots and send down into a sphere of forgotten ideas. When he has thus selflessly torn from himself what his soul had previously generated and has handed it over to the world outside himself, then it will return to him as Inspiration.' (GA 62)

must, as it were, stretch forth spiritual organs through which we may regain spiritual reality. If we more and more live our way into a soul life of this kind, we shall become ever increasingly connected with the beings and things of the spiritual world. What will then enter into our consciousness is that we no longer associate with those beings in the way one person associates with another by means of external organs; we will experience these beings directly through being not outside them but within them. That is when Intuition comes about which is actually the height of supersensible knowledge, that spiritual knowledge which leads us not into some vague, nebulous spiritual life but into a concrete life of spiritual form filled with reality. There is no other way of genuinely meeting with the spirit and its existence than by blending entirely with it in the manner just described. Something with which we do not blend can never be valid as a proof of the spirit, for there is no other proof than that of finding one's own experience as being identical with an experience of the spirit. Whoever wishes to experience a spiritual being must bring his soul to the point where he can allow his own experience to be identical with the experience of that spiritual being.[94]

If we wish to recognize these creative beings who lie hidden behind all external existence, we must be capable of tearing our inner soul life out of ourselves as strongly as is the case when we have ascended to Intuition. In a concrete situation this means that it is exceedingly difficult to recognize the previous incarnation of an individual by means of supersensible insight because when we encounter an individual in the sense world we are also dealing with something which expresses itself in the workings of nature, in bodily influences.

Behind these bodily influences there lies something resembling creative powers. But for the spiritual seer this is hidden behind the workings of the body, just as the spiritual beings who exist behind lightning and thunder and the whole of nature are also hidden behind these things; the one is scarcely easier to find than the other. That is why it frequently happens that individuals who reach Intuition tell of all kinds of things, genuine illusions from their former incarnations. That is why it is good to pay as little attention to this as possible. The true spiritual seeker knows that this is one of the most difficult aspects which even for the most highly developed soul is possible only momentarily.[95]

In order to enter fully into the spiritual world one must immerse oneself in things, one must become one with the things of the spiritual world. This occurs in *Intuition*, the third stage of spiritual knowledge. So the spiritual researcher enters into the realm of the spiritual world through Imagination, Inspiration and Intuition. With Intuition he stands in the spiritual world in such a way that his own self of spirit and soul has become independent of all that is bodily, as described in more detail in *Knowledge of the Higher Worlds*, and he has immersed himself in the spiritual beings of the world in so far as he is capable of this. Thus have we characterized what may be termed the relationship of spiritual research to the spiritual world, an experience of the spiritual through feeling oneself to be at one with the beings and processes of the spiritual world. This is what must be understood as that which characterizes spiritual science.[96]

Still more mature—and what constantly develops does indeed become ever more mature—is what lives in us when it no longer needs to be only Inspiration but can be Intuition in the sense in which I use this word in my *Knowledge of the Higher Worlds*. But Intuition can only be a being who has solely a single 'spirit body', if I may use such a paradoxical expression. A human being can only influence others intuitively, including those who still live in a physical body, once he has laid his astral body aside, once he himself belongs wholly to the spiritual world—in other words, decades after he has died. When that time comes he can, as I have described, work down into other individuals no longer solely through Inspiration. Then, as an I now living in the spiritual world, he works in a spiritual way upon their I. Formerly he worked through Inspiration into their astral body, or into their etheric body via the detour of his etheric body. Decades after his death an individual can also work directly, of course also mediated by others. His individuality has now become so mature that he can enter livingly not only into the habits of others but also into their contemplations! In view of today's prejudiced sentiments, this may even be an awkward, indeed a rather distasteful truth; but a truth it is, nevertheless. Our contemplations, which arise in our I, are constantly being influenced by those who have died long ago. Those who died long ago live in our contemplations. Through this the continuity of evolution is maintained out of the spiritual world. This is a necessity, and if it were not so, the thread of contemplations would constantly be broken off.[97]

Intuition is a word which is constantly used in ordinary life, although there it denotes a less clear and more emotional form of knowing. This type of intuition, about which we often speak and which is a less clear form of knowing, is not what is meant by the spiritual researcher when he talks of Intuition. Nevertheless there is some justification for thinking that the underdeveloped obscurity of what is ordinarily meant by intuition might be a kind of preliminary stage of what is reached by true Intuition. True Intuition is then just as much a way of inward knowing and feeling of soul permeated by an inner clarity of awareness as—once again I am obliged to refer to mathematics—as is mathematical thinking.[98]

The inner being reveals itself to us as we pour ourselves with loving devotion into something that inspires us. And when, livingly exalted like this, we experience the reality of spirit and soul, then we are within Intuition.

This is intuitive knowledge. Shades of Intuition are already present in ordinary life, and these shades of Intuition are alive in religious experience, in religious feeling. Whatever is purely inward in religious feeling, without our having entered into a specific world, is in spiritual Intuition filled with utter reality. Thus spiritual Intuition is similar and yet utterly different from purely religious feeling. Purely religious feeling remains subjective. In spiritual Intuition the inner being streams into objectivity and inhabits the reality of spirit and soul, so that one can say: The intuitive way of supersensible knowing is similar to, but also dissimilar from, religious knowing.[99]

It is not necessary for everybody to find a way livingly into the divine-spiritual world through Intuition. But someone who is to become a spiritual researcher will be obliged to do so. When the spiritual researcher expresses in words ... what he experiences in the divine, spiritual world, then this takes on a form which, when revealed in this way, is consciously experienced by ordinary individuals. Words are spoken which do not refer to the ordinary world, but through the reality of the power within them they come to life within the human soul. And this is the power which shows to people's consciousness, in a religious way, what spiritual research brings down through the intuitive experience of the spiritual, divine world.[100]

If humanity is to find its way once more to an original religious life founded upon insight, then validity will have to be accorded to what the spiritual researcher is able to tell of his experiences of the divine, spiritual world attained through true Intuition. Then will religion return once more to what it originally was. Every religion was at its starting point a revelation from the divine, spiritual world, a revelation of those experiences which can be attained together with the beings of the spiritual world, with those beings who initially reveal themselves through imaginative and inspired knowledge but with whom one can only meet truly through Intuition.[101]

If an individual wishes to proceed further, he will have to add to Imagination and to his empty consciousness a third faculty of knowledge, a faculty of knowledge which in today's view of understanding is very frequently not regarded as a faculty of knowledge at all, a faculty which plays the greatest possible role in human life but is not regarded as having the right to contribute to knowledge in any way. This is the human power of love—that love which unites an individual with others through the way in which he approaches the being he loves through the physical body or through the soul or spirit embodied therein; through the further cultivation of this love so that it can reach into an experience, initially, of the etheric body but can then also be brought into an experience of the astral body. Through a further development of this faculty for love we then finally reach the ability not only to experience our physical body but also, after a while, to enhance that love to such an extent that we not only see other spiritual beings— we ourselves are by then spiritual—but become able to relate to them in the same way as we were able to relate to physical human beings on earth. Intuition enables us to relate to spiritual beings in the same way as we are able to relate to physical human beings on earth. Once we have cultivated our capacity for love to such an extent that what is spiritual becomes just as objective to us as are sense-perceptible things in the physical world, then we succeed not only in looking back into our pre-earthly existence but also into our former lives on earth. It then becomes a fact for us that we go through our entire human life in forms of existence between birth and death and then between death and a new birth, and again from birth to death, and again from death to a new birth, thus living our life through sequential lives on earth and in sequential spiritual lives. We learn to look back to our former life on earth and see the present life as a repetition of that earlier one.

But no one can reach a view of what he was like, or what he was, or that he existed at all in an earlier life, unless he has been able to cultivate love up to a stage in which he can stand before himself just as he stands before another being. There must be an almighty difference between our ordinary earthly faculties and those faculties of knowledge infused with love through which we view our earlier life on earth like the life of another person in the present. When we have reached the stage which I have termed the intuitive stage, the truly intuitive stage, then we see ourselves in repeated earthly lives standing before our spiritual eyes as beings who are spiritually active. Then are we fully outside our bodily life. And someone who experiences this knows what death is. Death then stands before him as the external, objective realization of that which he himself has accomplished through knowledge. Having become aware of laying aside his physical and his etheric body, he now knows that death is only a laying aside of the physical and etheric body and that the human being passes through the portal of death into a spiritual world. Belief becomes knowledge, opinion becomes understanding. What we otherwise speak of in life as immortality becomes a sure, exact, evident knowledge. We look at the immortality of our own human life, at the entry of this, our own human being, into a life after death; we look at a pre-birth life in the spirit, a pre-earthly life.

But we also see what has evolved in physical life on earth

between people in their physical life by way of relationships within the family, where one individual relates to another, and how relationships of love, of friendship come about in human life. We see all this. Just as in death the physical body falls away from the individual while the soul rises up into the spiritual world, so does what is physical on earth in relationships of friendship, of love fall away, becoming a soul-filled, much more intimate co-habitation than when here on earth individuals were brought together through their destiny, so that once they have passed through the gate of death they find one another again among higher beings. Modern initiation can only show what the path is like in order that one may see what for knowledge is immortality, the other side of eternity.

Thus does the human being rise through imaginative knowledge to seeing what lives between birth and death. When he reaches this knowledge, the human being rises up to his etheric body. Inspired knowledge then leads the human being to his astral body and he thus enters into the world which he traversed prior to birth and into which he enters once again after death. In the astral body one learns to know the human being's pre-earthly and post-mortem sphere of life. Rising up to Intuition one comes to know the fourth member of the human being, the true and eternal I which journeys from earthly life to earthly life and which has a purely spiritual existence between those lives on earth.[102]

5. Intuition Exercises

If something is to be done concerning the attainment of knowledge through Inspiration, it is impossible to over-emphasize the fact that initially all forms of interest in ordinary life that manifest as likes and dislikes regarding truth and untruth must first be silenced so that an entirely different form of interest can come about which is devoid of any kind of self-interest. However, this characteristic of the inner life of soul is only one among the means that can prepare for Inspiration. There are untold numbers of others which must be added to this one. And the further the spiritual observer refines what has served him for Inspiration, the closer will he be coming to Intuition.[103]

The exercises leading to Intuition make it necessary for the pupil of the spirit to remove from his awareness not only the images to which he turned in order to attain Imagination but also what he practised in his life of soul for the attainment of Inspiration. He must have absolutely *nothing* in his soul of any previous external or internal experiences. However, if *nothing* were to remain in his consciousness after he has cast off his external and internal experiences, that is if his con-sciousness were to disappear altogether, this would show him that he is not yet sufficiently mature for the exercises necessary for the attainment of Intuition; so he would need to continue with the exercises for Imagination and Inspiration. The moment will eventually come when his consciousness is not empty after his soul has eliminated those internal and external experiences; then, after such elimination, something will continue working in his consciousness in which he will be able to immerse himself in the same way as he immersed himself in what he owes to external or internal impressions. This 'something', however, is of a very special kind. Over against all previous experiences it is something truly new. When this experience arises, one knows: This is something I previously did not know. This is a perception just as a genuine sound is a perception heard by the ears; but this something can only enter into my consciousness through Intuition, just as the sound can only enter into my consciousness through my ears. Through Intuition the final remnant of what is sense-perceptible and physical is removed from the human being's impressions; the spiritual world begins to open up to one's knowledge in a form that no longer has anything in common with the attributes of the physical, sense-perceptible world.[104]

Now the pupil of the spirit eliminates even his own activity of soul from his consciousness. Of what remains, there is *nothing* that cannot be comprehended. Nothing can become enmeshed in it that cannot be comprehended with regard to its content. So the pupil of the spirit possesses something in his Intuition which shows him the utterly clear reality of how the world of spirit and soul is constituted. If he then applies what he recognizes as the real characteristics of spirit and soul to everything he observes, then he is able to distinguish between appearance and reality. And he can then rest assured that if he applies this law he will be protected against illusions in the supersensible world just as in the physical, sense-perceptible world it is impossible for him to mistake an *imagined* piece of hot iron for one that can actually burn him. Obviously one will only react in this way to knowledge which one regards as arising solely from one's own experiences in the supersensible world, and not as one does to what is received as information in the physical world which one comprehends through one's own healthy feeling for what is true. The pupil of the spirit will make every effort to make a clear distinction between what he has acquired either in the one way or in the other way. He will on the one hand be prepared to accept information he is given about the higher worlds and to understand it on the basis of his own competence to judge. But if he himself learns something through his own experience which he judges to have been observed by himself, then he will recognize what has thus come towards him as being an infallible Intuition.[105]

One endeavours, for example, to imagine processes of the physical world that follow a specific course, by proceeding backwards from the end to the beginning. In doing this one removes one's soul life, by means of a will-process which in ordinary consciousness one does not apply, from the cosmic outer content and enters with it directly into those beings who reveal themselves through Inspiration. One attains *genuine Intuition*, namely a cohabitation with beings in a spiritual world.[106]

Through this *intuitive knowing* one becomes able to see the true being of the I which is in reality immersed within the spiritual world. What is present of the I in ordinary consciousness is merely a feeble reflection of its true form. Through Intuition one becomes able to sense this feeble reflection as being united with the divine archetypal world to which it truly belongs. One can thus also see how the spiritual human being, the true I, exists in the spiritual world when the individual is absorbed in sleep. In this state the physical and the etheric organisms use the rhythmical processes for themselves, for the purpose of their regeneration. In the state of wakefulness the I lives in this rhythm and in the physical metabolic processes incorporated within it. In the state of sleep the human being's rhythms and the metabolic processes live their own life in the physical and etheric organism; and the astral organism and the I have their own existence in the spiritual world. Through inspired and intuitive knowledge the human individual is brought *consciously* into that world. He lives within a spiritual cosmos in the same way as he lives in a physical cosmos through his senses.[107]

In addition to what has been described thus far, the following soul exercise also leads to Intuition. One endeavours to intervene in life, which has thus far progressed unawares from one age to the next, by developing habits one has not previously had or by transforming those habits which one has had. The greater the efforts needed to bring about such a transformation, the better it is for bringing about intuitive knowledge. These transformations bring about a disengagement of the forces of will from the physical and etheric organism. One binds the will to the astral organism and to the true form of the I and thus *consciously* immerses both of these into the spiritual world.[108]

In Intuition, by means of will exercises ... the human individual is taken with his consciousness into the objective world of cosmic beings. He will reach a state of experience originally possessed only by archetypal human beings. They were united with their cosmic surroundings in the same way as they were with the processes of their own bodies. *Those* processes were not entirely in the unconscious as they are nowadays for present-day human beings. They were mirrored in the soul. The individual experienced his growing, his metabolism in his soul as though in waking dreams. And what he experienced in this way enabled him, as though dreaming, to experience the processes of his cosmic surroundings and what was spiritually within them. He possessed a dreamlike Intuition of which only an echo is nowadays present in some individuals who are fittingly gifted. In the awareness of original human beings their surroundings were both physical and spiritual. What was half dreamingly experienced was for an original human being a religious revelation. For him it was a direct continuation of his life as a whole. What for an original human being were dreamlike experiences in the spiritual world remain entirely unconscious for present-day individuals. But someone with intuitive knowledge can bring them into full consciousness. And he is thus taken back in a new way to the condition of archetypal humanity for whom awareness of the world still possessed a religious content.

Just like a philosopher compared with a child, or a cosmologist compared with a fully aware individual of a former middle epoch of humanity, so will one who has religious knowledge in the modern sense come to resemble once more the archetypal human being, except that now he experiences the spiritual world in his soul not as though in a dream but in full consciousness.[109]

Now comes a task which is the opposite of the task of a mystic. What we have to do is similar to ordinary science: we must go into the outside world. This is what is difficult, but it is necessary if intuitive knowledge is to come about. The person must turn his attention away from his own activity.... If he has patience, if he carries out his exercises long enough and correctly, then he will see that something remains with him of which he is entirely certain that it is absolutely independent of his own inner experience. It is not tinged subjectively; it leads him upwards to something which is independent of his subjective personality but which shows by its objective quality that it is the same as the centre of one's being, the centre of the human I. If we want to reach this in intuitive knowledge, we go out of ourselves and yet come to something that is identical with our own inner being. In this way we ascend from what we experience inwardly to what is spiritual, which we now experience not within ourselves but in the external world.[110]

We encounter especially what is necessary in this connection when we approach Intuition through which the soul, that has become a spiritual researcher, is able to place itself into the inner being of another spiritual being or another spiritual fact. We shall come to realize that it becomes impossible, in accordance with spiritual schooling, to enter truly into another being if one has not, already here in the physical world, made sure that one has an open interest for all that is around one, a free and open interest. Every narrow-minded reserve of the soul, every hiding away of the soul within itself, everything that does not turn the attention of the soul towards sharing in suffering and sharing in enjoyment with its fellow creatures and especially with what already surrounds us in the world of sense, all this prevents the soul, once it has risen up into the spiritual world, from attaining true Intuition, true recognition of higher beings.[111]

The appropriate preparation for an intuitive knowledge here in the physical world is one which as far as possible strengthens the soul and accustoms it to being interested in everything that lives and breathes and is, to being able to pay attention to whatever surrounds it. The greater the depth of our interest can be, the better shall we be prepared, as spiritual researchers, to have an Intuition of higher worlds. Therefore we can say: Especially for spiritual science it becomes obvious that the shining of sympathy for the physical world resembles a reflection of those profound forces of the soul which lead to Intuition; and these can only develop truly and correctly if the soul prepares itself, in genuine interest for its environment, through loving it and feeling sympathy for it.[112]

Again and again we find, expressed in various writings, that an individual who has been brought, through the mysteries, to an experience of the spiritual world and its processes and beings, has arrived at the 'gate of death'. This means that he experiences something of which he knows immediately that it resembles the experience of death or that it is something which, if one understands it, can show one what death is. Someone going through initiation knew that he would have to go right up to the frontier of death. This is what has always been said. And in my book *A Way of Self-Knowledge* I was obliged to describe an experience that I have also mentioned here, which a person has when for many years he allows those exercises to work on him which we call meditation, concentration and so on. What I said was: When an individual undertakes to develop his soul in such a way that it briefly leaves his body and has a body-free experience, then he arrives at an infinitely significant moment, a moment which deeply affects his soul when it occurs for the first time. For a spiritual researcher this must happen frequently; but when it occurs for the first time it is a most profound experience for the soul. When one intensifies to its limits a soul activity that in ordinary life is described as paying attention, then the powers of soul which are independent of the body increase to such an extent that a specific moment arises in the soul's life. It can occur in the midst of the bustle of everyday life; and it does not even have to worry one if one has undergone a proper preparation such as I have described in my book *Knowledge of the Higher Worlds*. If one arrives at an experience of this kind, ordinary daily life can proceed as normal. Or it can come about in the depths of one's night-time experiences, in sleep. One suddenly feels, also in daily life, how an Inspiration or an Intuition streams into ordinary life. I want to describe what is typical about this. It can occur in hundreds of different ways, but there will always be one specific aspect which I now want to describe. I want to try and put it into words; but in doing this I realize that it can only be inadequately described in words that are borrowed from sense-perceptible life.

One feels as though one is being rudely awakened from sleep and one has a feeling that something is asking: What is happening to me? It feels like lightning striking in the room where one finds oneself and as though it were smashing the vessel of one's external bodily nature. In such a moment of heightened awareness one feels not only that something is approaching one which will destroy one in one's external bodily nature, but also that one is being permeated and pulsed through by whatever it is that wants to destroy one's external bodily nature. One feels that in this experience one can only remain upright with the help of strengthened inner soul forces, and one says to oneself: Now I know all about what can exist in the external world that wants to separate me from the bodily nature I inhabit. From that moment onwards one knows, through what one has experienced in this way, that there exists within the spirit and soul of the human being something which in every way is independent of one's bodily nature, and that this bodily nature has been developed for one as an external receptacle and tool.

From that moment on one has an image of what death is. Initially, however, it is indeterminate knowledge, an indeterminate experience; but it gives the soul the feeling, the inner grasp of a spiritual reality, which enables it to come to grips with what makes it capable of penetrating into the realms of spiritual life. This experience, about which I have spoken, is an intimate one, but it is an experience that is human in a general way because it is so serious that it releases one in the narrower sense from what is connected with one's personal wishes and will, and which acquaints one with what otherwise always lies hidden behind life as such.[113]

Through the increase in attentiveness and dedication brought about by exercises practised within the soul, the human individual becomes aware inwardly of how those forces live within him which raised him into uprightness as a child. He becomes conscious of spiritual guiding forces of uprightness and of movement, and as a result he becomes able to add to the inner physiognomy of his spirit and soul also his inner mimicry, his inner expressiveness, his inner gesturing motions, his inner gesticulations. When his spirit and soul are thus distanced from the physical, bodily nature in this way, when the individual, as a spiritual researcher, begins to comprehend the meaning of the words, 'you are experiencing yourself in the realm of spirit and soul'—then the time has also arrived in which he becomes aware of those forces which have raised him up, which have placed him vertically upon the earth as a bodily, sensual being. He now uses these forces purely in the realm of spirit and soul and he thus becomes able to use them in a way that differs from his use of them in ordinary life. He becomes able to give these forces a different direction, so that now he can form himself in a way that differs from his physical experience during his childhood. He now knows how to develop inner movements, how to adapt to all directions; he knows how to give other physiognomies to his spirit than those that are possible as an earthly human being; he becomes able to immerse himself in other spiritual procedures and beings; he can connect in such a way that he can take those forces which transformed him from a crawling infant into a vertically upright individual and transform them yet again within spiritual things and beings so that he comes to resemble those things and beings, thereby giving expression to them and thus becoming able to perceive them. This is genuine Intuition. For true perception of spiritual beings and processes is an immersion into them, an adoption of their own physiognomy. When one experiences, through one's own inner mimicry, the processes taking place within the beings, when one experiences the movements of spiritual beings through becoming capable of imitating their gestures, then one is able to convert oneself into those things and beings through taking on the actual forms of the spirit, then one perceives that one has oneself become spirit.[114]

The great difference between knowledge of the spirit and ordinary knowledge of what is external is that external knowledge adapts passively to things whereas spiritual knowledge must live in perpetual activity, so that the human being must become that which he wishes to perceive.[115]

This Intuition is especially attained through a continuation of what I termed the exercises for the attainment of forgetting. These exercises must be carried out in such a way that forgetting becomes a kind of un-egoistic forgetting of oneself. When these exercises are carried out with systematic precision, something arises which in this higher sense is termed Intuition by the spiritual researcher. It is that form of knowing to which inspired Imagination ultimately leads.[116]

6. Three Stages of Consciousness—Intuition in Relation to Imagination and Inspiration

In spiritual science this *first* stage of knowledge is termed 'material knowledge'. To this are then added *three* higher forms of knowledge. Others subsequently also follow.... If we regard the ordinary—sense-perceptible—stage of knowledge as the first, we then distinguish, initially, between four stages:

1. Material knowledge,
2. Imaginative knowledge,
3. Inspired knowledge, which may also be termed 'will-knowledge',
4. Intuitive knowledge.

...It is initially necessary to reach an understanding of what is involved in these various forms of knowledge. In the ordinary knowledge of sense-perception, four elements have to be considered: 1. the *object* which makes an impression on the senses; 2. the *image* which one has of this object; 3. the *concept* through which one reaches a mental comprehension of a thing or a process; 4. the *'I'* which forms for itself an image and a concept of the object.[117]

The various stages of higher knowledge ... may then be described as follows:

1. The study of spiritual science in which one initially applies one's power of judgement gained in the physical, sense-perceptible world.
2. Attaining the knowledge of Imagination.
3. The reading of the hidden script (as in Inspiration).
4. Familiarizing oneself with one's spiritual environment (as in Intuition).
5. Understanding the conditions of microcosm and macrocosm.
6. Becoming one with the macrocosm.
7. The overall experience of the preceding experiences as a fundamental mood of soul.

However, it is not necessary to think that one must proceed through these stages consecutively. Schooling can take place in such a way that, depending on the individuality of the spirit pupil, a preceding stage may be passed through, only perhaps to a specific point, before he begins to practise the exercises belonging to the next stage. It may, for example, be quite useful first to gain some Imaginations in a reliable way while at the same time practising exercises that allow one also to gain one's own experiences of Inspiration, of Intuition or of a knowledge of the connections between microcosm and macrocosm.[118]

The content of spiritual vision can only be reproduced in images (Imaginations) through which Inspirations speak which stem from Intuitions of spiritual existence.[119]

Moral impulses as such are real because they originate in the spiritual world; the way in which the individual experiences them in his world of appearances enables him to define himself *freely* in accordance with them, or not to define himself at all. *They themselves* do not coerce him in any way either through his body or through his soul.

Humanity progresses in such a way that the thinking of olden times—which was entirely bound up with unconscious imagined, inspired and intuitive knowledge, and in which thoughts were *revealed* as Imagination, Inspiration and Intuition—becomes abstract thinking that is carried out by the physical organism. In *this* thinking, which has an apparent life of its own because it is spiritual in substance but has been transplanted into the physical world, the human being has the possibility of developing an objective knowledge of nature and also his own moral freedom.... But in order to enter once more into a philosophy, a cosmology and a religion that embraces the whole human being, it is necessary to enter *consciously*—as opposed to the old dreamlike clairvoyance— into the realm of exact clairvoyance in Imagination, Inspiration and Intuition. In the realm of abstract conceptual life the human being becomes fully conscious. As humanity progresses it is up to the individual to carry this full consciousness into his experiences of the spiritual world. This is what genuine human progress must come to be, on into the future.[120]

It is precisely in this experience of being awake, which comes about here ... that the impulse lies for moving on from the sequences of dreaming and being awake to that other sequence which I have described with regard to Imagination, Inspiration and Intuition. The transitional steps experienced are just as abrupt as those between dreaming and being awake; and from the point of view of exact Imagination, Inspiration and Intuition, what occurs when one is awake possesses characteristics of reality which, when seen from the point of view of wakefulness, are not present in dreaming.[121]

An individual's moral attitude to life depends upon his moral views, upon his moral understanding of other individuals, and upon his moral powers. Thus it is solely out of the cultivation of moral insights that Imagination can evolve, that receptivity for Inspiration can come about out of the practice of moral understanding, and that Intuition can be developed out of the cultivation of moral powers. That is why one to whom Imaginations are described can develop moral insight, while one who hears about Inspirations develops moral understanding and one who is told about Intuitions develops moral strength. In this way communication about such insights approaches the source of what is moral within the human being.[122]

We shall gradually come to know how that which leads human beings up into the supersensible world proceeds along three paths. When speaking about these three paths we may find ourselves in danger of being regarded as dreamers by some and, especially when describing the third path, as utter imbeciles even though those who reach such conclusions have no idea what they are talking about. We are shown three paths: Imagination or clairvoyance, Inspiration and Intuition. These three paths have existed for millennia throughout human evolution, and they have been trodden since time immemorial. There have always been individuals who have been permitted to enter into the supersensible worlds through being taught by means of the methods described.[123]

1. In pure thoughts you find
   the self which can maintain itself.

2. When you change the images into thoughts
   you experience creative wisdom.

3. When you condense feeling into light
   you reveal the forming power.

4. When you make a real being of the will
   you are creative in world existence.

These four mantras show the stages of higher knowledge in sequence. Thus, depicted

in the 1st mantra is pure thinking through which we
   comprehend the I,
in the 2nd mantra is Imagination (image)
in the 3rd mantra is Inspiration (light)
in the 4th mantra is Intuition (being).

Practised in this way they lead the pupil from thinking into the very being of the spirit itself.[124]

The knowledge and research which lead us into these realms are, as you all know, not something that has only now, in our time, entered into human evolution; there exists what we might call a wisdom of the archetypal world. Whatever human beings can fathom, whatever human beings can know and recognize, whatever they can achieve by way of concepts and ideas, whatever they can achieve in the form of the Imaginations and the Inspirations and the Intuitions of clairvoyance, all this is of course only experienced in hindsight by human beings; it has been experienced with foresight, known with foresight, by the higher beings who reign above humanity. Using a rather trivial comparison we might say: Initially the clockmaker has the idea of the clock and then, in accordance with this, he manufactures the clock. The clock is made in accordance with the clockmaker's thought which preceded it, and subsequently someone can take the clock to pieces, analyse it and study the thoughts of the clockmaker who made it. Such a person is then thinking the thoughts of the clockmaker with hindsight. This is the only way, at the present stage of our evolution, in which we can study the primeval wisdom of the spiritual beings who stand above us. They were the first to have the Imaginations, the Inspirations, the Intuitions, the ideas and the thoughts in accordance with which our world, as it lies before and around us, was brought into existence. And human beings now find these thoughts and ideas in this world. And when they raise themselves up into clairvoyant seeing, there they find the Imaginations, the Inspirations, the Intuitions through which they can once again enter into the world of the spiritual beings. So we can say: Prior to our world there existed the wisdom about which we are intending to speak. This is the plan of the world.[125]

That was also, in those more ancient times, the path along which the human individual searched for his wisdom, along which he searched for a higher form of knowledge about the world than what could be found behind the tapestry of the external world of the senses. The individual searched by means of immersing himself in his own internal world. Out of this internal world further Intuitions and Inspirations of moral and ethical life had to rise up, just as Intuitions of conscience also rose up out of that internal world. All other Intuitions and Inspirations relating to morality and the soul as such also rose up as a matter of course out of the soul realm. That is why those higher individualities who were the leaders of humanity in those ancient times, and who needed to bring about enlightenment regarding the highest matters, had to address themselves to the inner human being. It was to the soul life of the human being, to the human being's inner life, that the holy Rishis and the great teachers of humanity had to address themselves.[126]

What Goethe in those days initially meant ... by 'the perceptive power of judgement' is in a certain sense the beginning of today's no longer unknown upward path of knowledge. As we shall see, spiritual science will be in a position to point towards the fact that hidden powers of knowledge exist which proceed upwards in various stages and thus enter ever further into the spiritual world.

When we speak of knowledge we initially mean knowledge of the everyday world, 'objective knowledge'; and then we speak of 'imaginative knowledge', whereby the word 'imaginative' is used as a technical term, just as are also the others; we speak of 'inspired knowledge', and finally of true 'intuitive knowledge'. These are stages of development passed through by the soul on its way to the supersensible

world. But they are also, in the sense of today's soul constitution, stages of soul development passed through by the
spiritual researcher. Spiritual researchers in ancient times
travelled along similar paths.[127]

Thus we are also able to point out that Intuition, too, has a
specific relationship with our feelings. That is why mystics,
prior to reaching any clearly defined notions about the higher
worlds, enter into a kind of generalized experience of them in
their feelings, and many are quite satisfied with this; indeed,
many are satisfied with even less. But those who become
properly immersed in the higher worlds with their feeling life
do then all describe in the same way the state of devotion in
their souls. In other words, there are what one might describe
as all kinds of feeling relationships to be found in a direct
experience of the spiritual world.

If we then wanted to proceed further through this Intuition, which plays a role in our feelings, we would be unable to
do so because there is then a need to proceed more from the
other direction. In order not to luxuriate in such feelings but
instead in order to reach a concrete view of the spiritual
world, we must endeavour to form Imaginations and turn
our attention to these with regard to the spiritual world.
Then, gradually, a connection will form in our life between
the as yet not understood but more feelingly experienced
Intuition and the still rather unreal Imagination, floating in
unreality, which consists only of pictures. What brings about
the connection here helps us to approach the thought that we
have now come close to the beings who bring about what
happens spiritually. This coming close to those beings is

termed Inspiration. In a certain way this is the opposite of the processes which occur with regard to the external, physical world. In this world we have, as it were, those thoughts which we form about things; here, the things are presented to us and we form thoughts about them. There, though, what happens is that the thing which initially appears in our feelings, is utterly indeterminate, and an Imagination as such would, as it were, be floating in mid-air. Only when the two come together, when Imagination works through Inspiration into Intuition, when, in other words, our ideas lead us up to Imagination and when we feel that the Imagination is something which comes from beings, then the essence of those beings flows into us as an event. Something is brought through the Imagination which streams in out of the Intuition and so we perceive through this event a content which may be compared with the content of thoughts. We then perceive these thoughts, for the perception of which we have prepared ourselves through Imagination, in what is given to us through what happens in Intuition.[128]

This departure from Paradise does indeed show how the human being was originally in the spiritual world, that is in Paradise, where he consisted of Imagination, Inspiration and Intuition, which means in an entirely super-earthly existence.[129]

Through his bony system the human being continuously brought forth Imaginations, through his muscular system he continuously sent Inspirations out into the world, and through his nervous system Intuitions.[130]

Everywhere, underlying human cultures, one finds hidden an original knowledge, a knowledge out of Intuition, Inspiration and Imagination.[131]

When the human being enters into the spiritual world through Imagination, through Inspiration and through Intuition, he meets there the master-builder, the creative being who works upon us before our consciousness arises, who builds the human body where we would as yet be unable to work because that work goes into the more delicate organization and the more delicate formation of the body.[132]

Everything we do, everything that must be brought about by us in the spiritual world, can only come about if we create the utmost quietude; but if we truly want to recognize anything at all in the spiritual world we must then be uninterruptedly active. That is why, for some who would like to be anthroposophists, what we do here out of genuine, true knowledge feels too uncomfortable. A good many say: With you, one has to learn everything first, one has to think everything through first, one has to concern oneself with everything!—But without this one does not reach an understanding of the spiritual world! One has to exert one's soul, one has to look at things from all angles. That is what it's all about. Concepts to be gained concerning higher beings must first be worked upon slowly and quietly. In the physical world if we want to have a table we must first produce it through our own energetic work. But if we want to 'produce' something in the spiritual world we must develop quietude, the kind of quietude which is needed if something is to come about; and if something does then come about it appears out of the twilight dusk. If we want to recognize something we must first create Inspirations by means of our utmost exertions. Recognizing something requires work, a soul mood that is inwardly active, a progress from Inspiration to Inspiration, from Imagination to Imagination, from Intuition to Intuition. Everything has to be brought together, and nothing that we want to recognize appears before us if we have not placed it here ourselves.[133]

The first stage of higher, of supersensible knowledge is what is called Imagination, imaginative knowledge.... The second stage of supersensible knowledge is Inspiration, and the third stage is what we ... might term true Intuition. The external or intellectual knowledge we possess in ordinary life, and also which we apply in the external sciences, is a kind of initial stage prior to these three stages of supersensible knowledge, so that when one includes it with the supersensible stages one can speak of four stages of human knowledge.

Now, there are many means, and many means must indeed be employed when one wants to raise oneself out of ordinary sensory and intellectual knowledge and up to the first stage of supersensible knowledge, Imagination ... One of these means is what is called meditation.[134]

Freedom is only made possible by what develops, independently of the external world, out of our thinking as an impulse for our actions.

Where do such impulses originate? Where is the origin of what does not come from the external world? Well, it originates in the spiritual world. There is no need for the individual to be clairvoyantly aware, in every situation in his life, of how these impulses come out of the spiritual world, yet they can nonetheless be within him. He will, however, need to comprehend them in a different way. When, in our seeing consciousness, we raise ourselves to the first stage of the spiritual world, that is the imaginative world; the second stage is the inspired world, as you know; the third stage is the intuitive world. So instead of raising up the impulse of our will, of our actions, out of our physical, out of our astral, out of our etheric body, we can, if we receive no impulses from that side but rather from the spiritual world, only receive them as Imaginations behind which stand Inspirations and Intuitions. But there is no need for this to be experienced consciously as clairvoyant consciousness, as 'This is what I now want, and behind it stand Intuitions, Inspirations and Imaginations.' Rather, the result appears as a concept, as pure thinking, and looks something like a concept brought about by phantasy.[135]

Only the human being has within him on earth something which is permanent. One cannot speak of the permanence of atoms, of substance, of force; one can only speak of the permanence of something within the human being. But this is only visible through Imagination, Inspiration and Intuition. Whatever else that cannot be seen in supersensible consciousness has no permanence.[136]

For human comprehension, logic as such contradicts life. That is why the human being is unable to form a living

concept if he wishes to base this concept purely on abstract
logic. Therefore the human individual can only form a
concept of what is alive if he is willing to rise up to Imagination, Inspiration and Intuition.[137]

But these two forces, that of Inspiration and that of Imagination, can unite with one another. The one can find its way
livingly into the other. But this must be done with full
awareness and through grasping hold lovingly of the cosmos.
Then what arises is a third element, a confluence of Imagination and Inspiration in genuine spiritual Intuition. In this
we rise up to a uniform recognition of the external world as a
spiritual world, an inward world of soul and spirit together
with its physical foundations, a recognition that teaches us
about the extension of human life over and above the life on
earth, as has been mentioned here, too, in other lectures.[138]

In external light a human being has a specific experience.
What is experienced by the individual through the sensory
perception of light in the external world is the same as what
he experiences in head-thinking with regard to Imagination.
One can therefore say: The element of thinking, seen
objectively, is seen as light, or rather is experienced as light.
In that we are human beings who think, we live in the light.
External light is seen by means of the physical senses; light
that becomes thinking is seen because one lives within it,
because one is oneself light as a thinking human being.
Initially one cannot see that which one is. But when one steps
outside the thinking, when one enters into Imagination and
Inspiration, then one confronts it, and then one sees the

element of thinking as light. So, with regard to the world as a whole, we can say: We have the light within us; only it does not appear to us as light because we are living within it, because by making use of light, by having light, it becomes thinking within us. You as it were make use of light; you take into yourself the light which otherwise appears to be outside you. You differentiate it within yourself. You work within it. That is what your thinking is; it is an action within the light. You are a being of light. You do not know that you are a being of light because you are living within the light. But the thinking which you develop, that is living in light. And when you look at thinking from the outside, then you do indeed see light.[139]

But when one is familiar with the process by means of which one arrives at such pure thinking, then through what becomes true, profound philosophy, something can be built up which I have described in various ways, as a method of knowledge of the higher worlds, in my book *Knowledge of the Higher Worlds* and in my *Outline of Esoteric Science*. Just as out of ordinary everyday activities of the human soul pure thinking arises for which no special schooling is required, so, by further developing this process, one can come to what I have termed the stages of higher knowledge in the book mentioned and in the second part of *An Outline of Esoteric Science*, namely Imagination, Inspiration and Intuition. What is expressed in pure thinking comes to belong to us human beings simply through our having been born. It has been handed down to us in our present stage of human evolution. What can become Imagination, Inspiration and Intuition must, in accordance with the example of pure thinking, be developed within the adult individual just as, in keeping with their nature, certain capabilities have to be taught to children.[140]

Imagination, Inspiration and Intuition are not intended to be something entirely foreign within human life which, as a foreign element, is supposed to lead to supersensible knowledge; they are entirely intended to belong within the ordinary sphere of human capabilities. Anthroposophy does not claim that some form of special conditions must be present that lead to Imagination, Inspiration and Intuition, but rather that the human being is capable of becoming conscious within more profound faculties which he is able to develop appropriately. There must be onward progress from the type of knowledge with which we are familiar through science in ordinary life and which we acquire in today's practical life.[141]

By means of certain exercises, carried out with an exactitude resembling that required for learning mathematics, one reaches the point at which one's powers of soul are such that one can leave one's physical body behind, not in a sleeping, unconscious way, not as in dreaming, but in full consciousness; the physical body, together with its intellectual thinking, is consciously left behind. One then has Imaginations which are not phantasies such as those that are justifiable in art, but which are, rather, expressions of the spiritual world as it is present all around us in today's world. Through Imagination, Inspiration and Intuition we learn to behold the spiritual beings of the spiritual world just as we see what is in the physical world. Just as our senses show us colours and sounds, so do we learn to look consciously in exact clairvoyance towards a spiritual world; not through hallucinations or illusions which always work on human beings by casting twilight over consciousness. We come to know the spiritual world with a consciousness that is as exact as is the consciousness applied in mathematics.[142]

And then, when one can dedicate oneself to this Inspiration, what comes about behind the worldly thoughts is the ability to perceive the world through Intuition. Imagination perceives pictures of the spirit, Inspiration hears the spirit speaking. Intuition perceives the beings themselves. I said that the world is filled with universal thoughts. These do not as such indicate the presence of any beings, but then we begin to hear words behind the thoughts and to see the beings of the world through Intuition.[143]

We already bear within us a part of the cosmos, but with our ordinary awareness we do not know this. By rising through Imagination, Inspiration, Intuition, right up to spiritual knowing, our inner experience in the soul becomes more and more sublime.[144]

7. Knowledge of Destiny—Intuition and Repeated Earth Lives

Only intuitive knowledge ... can enable us to carry out appropriate research into repeated lives on earth and into karma. All the knowledge that must be passed on as truth concerning those processes must come from research carried out through intuitive knowing. And if an individual wants to know himself in accordance with his own inner being, he can only achieve this through Intuition. Through this he can perceive what it is within him that advances from one earth life to the next.[145]

A consolidation of the life of soul ... adds to imaginative and inspired consciousness also that which is 'intuitive'. Through this it is possible to gain conceptions as to how spiritual forces, observable in one's destiny, which were at work in previous lives on earth, continue to work spiritually into the present.[146]

Through intuitive knowledge it is possible to reach conceptions regarding the way in which forces from past earth lives work on in the course of destiny. We shall here hint at the nature of these forces by means of a somewhat crude comparison. An experience in physical existence cannot be fully comprehended solely through what is observable in physical life. Its influence is far more comprehensive than what is directly experienced. There is also an effect on the soul which is initially not perceived consciously. This effect works on in the soul. It creates what may be approximately compared with an empty space among the soul forces. This 'emptiness' in the soul is carried through death and through the life between death and a new birth and continues to be present in the new life on earth. Here, spiritually—again in a somewhat crude comparison—it behaves in its surroundings like a space out of which all the air has been pumped but which has an opening to its surroundings. Through this the empty space sucks in the surrounding air. So the 'emptiness' sucks in the conditions of soul which are taking effect in the fabric of destiny. And because such 'emptinesses' continue to work once they have been created during a lifetime, it is possible for them to work on between an experience of one life and those that follow. So the soul itself creates connections between experiences of sequential earth lives. Out of its spiritual life between death and a new birth, and influenced by what occurred during the previous life, the soul takes a direction which creates connections with what originated previously.[147]

As a result of the development of Intuition through will exercises, it comes about that the previous earth life is revived in the sub-conscious. Through these will exercises the individual is brought into a state in which he enters into the world of the spirit outside his physical and etheric organism. He receives an experience of existence through becoming separated from his body. This gives him a preview of what will actually come about in death. This preview enables him to speak about the continuation of soul and spirit after the passage through death.[148]

Those soul exercises, when undertaken as will exercises with the aim of reaching supersensible vision, are only successful if they become an inward experience of pain. A feeling of suffering sets in for someone who raises his will to a higher level of energy. In former ages of human evolution this pain was brought about directly by ascetic exercises. They created a state in the body which made it difficult for the soul to approach it. The will-portion of the soul was thus torn away and became an independent experience of the spiritual world.

This type of exercise is no longer appropriate for the part of the human organization which has come into being during the present period of earth evolution. The human organism is now such that one prevents it from being the foundation for I-development when one practises the ancient exercises for asceticism. The opposite must now be practised. The soul exercises needed in the present time, in order to free the will-part of the soul from the body . . . strengthen this aspect of the soul not out of the bodily part but out of the soul part. They strengthen the soul and spirit aspect of the human being while leaving the physical and bodily aspect untouched.

Even in ordinary consciousness one can see how the experience of anguish is linked with the development of what is experienced in the soul. Anyone who has gained some degree of higher knowledge will say: I am grateful to destiny for the joyous and cheerful experiences in my life; but I owe my bitter and sorrowful experiences to my knowledge of life that is rooted in genuine reality.

If the will-part of the soul is to be strengthened in the way that is necessary for the attainment of intuitive knowledge,

then first of all the desires must be strengthened which are
lived to the full in ordinary human life by the physical
organism.... If these desires are such that the physical
organism in its earthly condition cannot provide a basis for
them, then the experience of the will-part of the soul passes
over into the spiritual world; and intuitive contemplation
comes into being. So for this form of contemplation the
spiritually eternal part of the soul's life becomes aware of
itself. Just as the consciousness living in the body experiences
that body, so does the spiritual consciousness experience the
content of a world of spirit.[149]

In the dreamless consciousness of sleep the human individual experiences his own being, without awareness, as
something permeated by the outcomes of former earth lives.
Inspired and intuitive consciousness presses forward to a
view of these outcomes and sees the effect of former earth
lives in the course (karma) of present destiny.[150]

The final period between death and a new birth is when the
soul chiefly undergoes its intuitive period. The first period
after death is the soul's imaginative period. Then gradually
the inspired period of the soul develops in full. Thereafter
there develops what gives the soul its entire individuality, the
soul-self, that which lives in Intuition, the capacity to open-
up within the other, to find a way into the other. What is it
into which the soul finds its way? What is it that chiefly intuits
it?

Already between death and a new birth the soul begins, at a
specific point, to feel a connection with the sequence of the

generations, and this leads to father and mother. Gradually the soul comes to feel connected with the ancestors, how they find one another in marriages, how they have children and so on. Immediately after death one feels the pictures, the unfolding of the pictures, so that as one looks down to the earth these pictures are brought together within greater imaginative correlations. And when one then turns once again toward life on earth one becomes more and more intuitive. On a greater scale the image I described yesterday comes before the soul: the globe of the earth—with a bluish tinge above Asia, India, East Africa; and on the other side— for we are of course circling round the earth—where America lies with a reddish glow; and between these the greenish and other tinges. And the earth also resounds with manifold notes: melodies, harmonies, choruses of the music of the spheres. And into this there emerge gradually the pictures one has had: the pictures one originally had of the sequence of the generations. Gradually one comes to recognize the thirty-sixth couple, the thirty-fifth couple of the ancestors, and then the thirty-fourth, and the thirty-third, and the thirty-second pair right down to father and mother. This is what one learns to recognize, woven into the Imaginations. Into these the Intuition imprints itself all the way to father and mother. This imprinting is really an opening up of what it is that lives in the generations. The second half of the life between death and a new birth is such that the human being becomes intensively accustomed to live in the other, in what is down there, already prior to that new life, and in the closer and also in the more distant surroundings, not in oneself but in what is other. One begins the life between death and a new birth by living in the other; the present life ends in such a way that one can live chiefly in the other. Then one is born, and one initially holds back something of this other life. That is why one must say that, during his first seven years, a human being is an imitator; he imitates everything he perceives. You can read about this in *The Education of the Child* [in GA 34]. It is the final imitation of that living-in-the-other which still continues on into physical life. That is the chief characteristic, transferred into the spiritual, of the life between death and a new birth, and it is the first characteristic to arise in a child: imitating everything there is. One will fail to understand this imitating in childhood if one does not know that it stems from the wonderfully intuitive life in spirit and soul of the final period between death and a new birth.[151]

During the final third [of the life between death and a new birth] one lives chiefly in Intuition, where the human being has to enter into his environment of soul and spirit. There he lives as though immersed with his consciousness in whatever is around him in soul and spirit. Especially during this final third, through such immersion, he is preparing himself to become immersed in the physical body after birth, or rather after conception. The Intuitions during the final third of the life between death and a new birth comprise that Intuition which consists, of course sub-consciously or unconsciously, in the human being immersing himself in the body which has been transmitted to him by the stream of inheritance from parents, grandparents and so on. And something of this remains once the individual has stepped across from the world of spirit and soul into the physical world. Considering

that the individual has been accustomed to living within
Intuitions of spirit and soul for long ages, it is understandable
that he wishes to remain within this familiarity once he has
entered into his physical body. So this is what he does. For
what is ... his chief endeavour of soul during his first seven
years of life up until the change of teeth?... A passion for
imitating. The child seeks to do whatever is being done
around him; he does not fulfil his own intentions; he enters
into the activities of those around him, copying whatever they
do. This is the echo of the Intuitions in which he lived during
the final third of his life between death and a new birth. We
are born as beings who imitate because we transfer into our
physical life what we have been doing for long ages in spirit
and soul in that other world. So we can understand why it is
that an individual grows into his body in this physical life
through harking back to what he was accustomed to doing in
the spiritual world.[152]

When the human being steps through the portal of death it
is the imaginative view that is initially rather strongly developed; a comprehensive world of pictures unfolds in Imaginations before him. This might be termed the unfurling of
the world of pictures. The second third of the life between
death and a new birth is chiefly filled with Inspirations. It is
Inspirations which arise during the second third of the
human being's life between death and a new birth; and
Intuitions during the final third. These Intuitions consist in
the human being entering with his self, with his soul
element, into other beings, and the end of these Intuitions
consists in his entering into the physical body. This enter-

ing into physical life through birth is simply a continuation of the chiefly intuitive life of the final third of living between death and a new birth. That which must happen when an individual enters into the physical realm is what is so characteristic of a child: he transplants himself into this other life. He is obliged to do what others do rather than what comes out of himself; he imitates, copies what others do.[153]

There really is a planned element in life. We could perhaps be mistaken about this. But I have only mentioned it because it is the most familiar way of looking at what arises out of intuitive knowing. Intuition surely does provide us with full insight not only into what goes on in the soul element of our organism but also into what is at work in us as our centre, our I, the true being of our self. This being of our self becomes visible through Intuition at the third stage of supersensible knowledge. It becomes visible because we do not confront the facts of the external world passively; we are drawn to them through what is given to us not through inheritance but through the profoundest being of our soul that has entered into us at birth out of a world of spirit and soul and taken on a physical, earthly body. Intuitive knowing teaches us that it enters into earthly life with an attitude that is not entirely passive, with regard to the facts it meets with, but that it is strongly attracted to some and strongly repelled by others. In short, it is born with the characteristics of its destiny within it.

And if one develops further this intuitive insight into the human being's self, then one comes to realize that the I has passed through repeated lives on earth. It is, however, the case that repeated earth lives began at a point in time when the I was so barely distinguishable from its environment that there was no such difference between an earthly life and a life of spirit and soul. There will be repeated lives on earth until a time comes when the I in its whole inner constitution so closely resembles the spiritual world that it will no longer need to undergo earthly lives.

So, in fully recognizing the I we recognize repeated lives on earth. In other words, we see that the overall life of the human being consists in there being parts of that life between birth and death, or conception and death, and other parts between death and a new birth; thus the human being accomplishes his entire life in repeated lives on earth.

We frequently hear the objection that the human individual does not remember those repeated lives on earth. But this only applies to our ordinary consciousness. As soon as Intuition comes about, however, what runs its course through repeated lives on earth is remembered inwardly in the soul just as a single earthly life is remembered in ordinary memory. So in this case, too, Anthroposophy reaches conclusions not through abstract proofs, as is the case with ordinary philosophy, but by first preparing the soul for higher knowledge which then enables the facts to be recognized. Thus this anthroposophical knowledge on the one hand proves to be a continuation of the knowledge attained through natural science while, at the same time, also being a continuation that must work in a way which differs utterly from what is merely the natural science we recognize nowadays.[154]

But what actually comes about within the true core of the human being can be discovered in advance through intuitive knowledge if, instead of being within one's physical body, one is out there in the world of the spiritual beings. For that is where one is. Through intuitive knowledge one is able, outside one's physical and etheric organization, to be within other spiritual beings in the same way as one is able, here on earth, to be within one's physical and one's etheric body. What one gains through Intuition is the image of an experience of what one has to go through in the event of dying. Only in this way can a true vision be acquired of what it is that underlies the immortal human soul. This human soul—as is already taught by inspired knowledge—is on the one hand unborn and on the other hand immortal.

This is what Intuition teaches us. What one comes to know in this way, through the eternal human core of being, insofar as it has to lead a life after physical death, this is what lies behind the human will. What lies behind human thinking ... can be recognized through Inspiration. What lies behind the human will can be recognized when one proceeds to Intuition by means of will exercises. In such a case the will is revealed to have behind it something quite other, of which the will of ordinary consciousness is merely a reflection. What is revealed is that there is something behind the will which is in a certain sense a younger member of human soul life. If we regard thinking and having ideas as something that is dying, indeed as something which is already dead, then we must regard the will as the younger part of the human soul. One might say that the will, or rather the soul element which lies behind the will, is related to thinking as a young child is related to someone who is well advanced in age.[155]

If we move on from here to Intuition and see how, out of the forming of the realm of the world-word, the world language, the human system of muscles and bones is woven, we then come to the first hierarchy, that of the Cherubim, Seraphim and Thrones. We have then more or less arrived at the moment between death and a new birth which lies in the middle, which I described in my mystery plays [GA 14] as the 'midnight hour of existence'. So we must then regard that which enables the human being to move about in the world as having been woven, begotten, created by the beings of the first hierarchy.[156]

Here is the human being in his current incarnation. When he develops Imagination, he sees his etheric body somewhat prior to birth or conception; but his astral body leads him through Inspiration into the entire time that has passed between his previous death and his current birth. And Intuition leads him back to his previous life on earth.[157]

8. Intuition in Practice—Examples From Various Specialist Fields

Geometry

In recent days I have already hinted at how we arrive at our customary geometrical constructions. We do not actually find them by means of abstractions derived from empirical ideas; rather, even mathematical and geometrical constructions are a form of Intuition. They are created out of the will-nature of the human being. As they have been created out of this, one can say that the human being, in grasping mathematical constructions, has in his experience gained at least some possibilities of working in, of finding reality in, the realm of mathematics. Even empirically they are a kind of interim position between the external realities, of which we can make pictures, and the direct content of existence which we experience inwardly. Thus, even an intellectual and empirical view would show that in comprehending geometry we find ourselves in an interim stage between prototype and likeness.[158]

Architecture

You will find it easy to convince yourselves—especially if you study Vitruvius—that the way in which one studied architecture in the past was very different from how one does this nowadays. One did not study it as we do today, by making calculations; rather, one received certain Intuitions that were expressed in symbols.... The way in which buildings were constructed in ancient times can no longer be imitated nowadays. Astonished and awe-struck we stand before Chinese buildings, or those of the Babylonians and Assyrians; yet we are aware that they knew nothing of today's mathematics. There is that wonderful work of engineering, the Lake of Moeris in Egypt; a lake that was constructed in order to collect water and, when needed, to send it out into the countryside along man-made canals. Its construction was not aided by today's knowledge of engineering. Also the wonderful acoustic qualities built into ancient buildings were created in ways of which today's architecture is still not capable. So, it was possible to build in ways that were intuitive rather than merely rational.

That entire way of building was related to knowledge about the universe as a whole. If you take the measurements of Egyptian pyramids you find they are linked with certain measurements of outer space, or the distances between the stars in the firmament. The entire configuration of the heavens was imitated in such buildings. There was a link between an individual building and the dome of heaven. That mysterious rhythm seen when gazing at the stars if we look not merely with our sensual eyes but with our intuitive eyes, that rhythm which is open to the rhythmical conditions of higher relationships, that is what those ancient architects built into their structures, for they built out of what they saw in the universe.[159]

Those cultural elements that stem from ancient times can only be understood if one comprehends them in connection with the sensations, with the feelings, with the Intuitions those people possessed regarding the spiritual world. One truly needs to have a sense of what the people felt who originally built the church surrounded by the graveyard. One must have a sense of the feeling they had. Beloved souls, who are departing from us, what forms do you wish that we should build for you so that while you still wing your way around your bodies, while you are still close to your bodies, you may find the forms which you wish to adopt after your death? And there it was, the answer that one wished to present to the questioning souls: the form of the church, the architecture of the church. Thus, at the end of earthly life, do we reach what is artistic in architecture.[160]

The Social Organism

The cultural life must not be wholly dependent upon the inner freedom of individuals; this cultural life must stand within the social organism in a way that is entirely free of rivalry. It must not rest upon any state monopoly. What it has gained through people's recognition can only arise on the basis of utterly free competition, on the basis of entirely voluntary accommodation towards the needs of society as a whole. (Its value for the individual is another matter, but we are concerned here with the needs of society as a whole.) Let anybody write poetry as much as he likes in his spare time, let him also find those who like his poetry; but what is fitting in cultural life is solely that which one wants to share with every other human individual. This, though, can only stand on a healthy foundation when all cultural life, all the life of schools and universities, all educational life and artistic life is removed from state monopoly and can stand on its own feet—although, as I have said, this cannot happen from one day to the next. The correct direction is given by allowing the individual to be responsible for himself. This is how the correct transition to something else can come about. Already in the 1890s I endeavoured in my book *The Philosophy of Freedom* to show how that which truly enables the individual to experience freedom can never be founded upon anything other than a true cultural life which plays into the soul of the individual. At the time I termed this the influence of Intuition in the human soul, the influence of what is genuinely cultural. This genuine culture must come to birth in the human soul in the light of freedom and of free competition, for then it will enter in the right way into the social organism. And then what is also important is that it must not be permitted to come under the supervision of any other section of the social organism; it must be able to reveal itself in utter freedom at the behest solely of what is generally needed.[161]

And the final [post-Atlantean] period would pre-eminently have the task of developing Intuition. Solely under the influence of this Intuition will it be possible for economic and industrial life as a whole to develop in the ideal sense of what such life really is.[162]

The concept of merchandise or goods may belong to the field of the economy, but it can never be modelled in accordance with ordinary science. You cannot arrive at the concept of merchandise or goods without founding it on imaginative knowledge. You can only grasp the concept of merchandise or goods if you found it upon imaginative knowledge. And you cannot understand work in the social, economic sense if you do not base it on inspired knowledge. And you cannot define capital without basing it on intuitive knowledge.

The concept of merchandise calls for Imagination,
The concept of work calls for Inspiration,
The concept of capital calls for Intuition.

And when these concepts are not formulated in this way, the result is always confused nonsense....

However, this does come about via a detour. The Bible points in a way to this detour by speaking of capitalism as 'Mammonism'. It thus links capital to a specific form of spirituality. But spirituality can only be recognized through Intuition. One needs Intuitions if one wants to recognize the spirituality, the 'Mammonism', that is at work in capitalism. This appeared already in the Bible. But today what we need is an understanding of the world which makes it properly modern.[163]

People will never in the future be so enthused by the enjoyment and love of work as they were in the past, when things were instinctive and atavistic, unless we permeate society with the ideas and sentiments that come into the world through the Inspiration of the initiates. These concepts must elevate people in such a way that they know: Before us we have the social organism and we must devote ourselves to it.

This means that work enters into their soul because they have an understanding of the social organism. Only those will reach such an understanding who have been told about inspired concepts, in other words about spiritual science. This means that, in order to bring about true work among humanity, what we need are not those empty concepts about which people shout nowadays, but rather spiritual sciences through which we may penetrate into hearts and souls. Then spiritual science will enter into hearts and souls in such a way that human beings will come to enjoy and love their work. Work will come to stand side by side with merchandise in a society that hears of images not only through those who are the pedagogues of society but also through Inspirations and through concepts which are necessary so that in our complicated society the means of production may come into being through which a proper basis can be created upon which people can work in suitable ways.

For this to happen the concepts of Intuition must be disseminated in our society. These concepts of capital, which you will find in my book *Towards Social Renewal* [GA 23], will only blossom in a society that is receptive for intuitive concepts. This means that capital will take its place in the social organism when one has once again admitted that it is important for Intuition to exist in the human being.[164]

And capital will only be properly utilized in the social organism when Intuition has risen up to freedom and when freedom will have blossomed out of a cultural life that develops itself. Then that which must flow from cultural life will flow into work.... And these three realms, once they have thus been formed, will come to intermingle in the right way.[165]

Education

Just as in the early years pleasure and delight helped to build the organs, so, from the seventh to the fourteenth—for boys to the sixteenth—year of life, is everything formed which brings about a sense of heightened health and joie de vivre; hence the value of lessons in gymnastics. However, this lacks value when the gym teacher regards his pupils from the point of view of an anatomist, when he aims solely at the external effect of a limb movement. It is far more important that the teacher should think his way intuitively into the child's feeling soul and that he knows which bodily movement gives the soul an impression of strength and health and allows the individual to feel well and happy within his own body. Only in this way can a gymnastic exercise gain inner value, or influence the feeling of developing strength. A true gymnastic exercise is of value not solely for appearances but also for the influence it has on the feeling human individual.[166]

Especially in the field of education the principle must take hold which shows that the human individual of today is inwardly essentially different from how he appears externally. This necessitates that in future teachers and educators should not be assessed as they are today but in accordance with quite different principles, for looking into the inner being of another person, which is not expressed outwardly, calls for a gift that is, in a way, prophetic. So it will become necessary to design the examinations for teachers in such a way that those with intuitive, prophetic gifts pass with especially high marks while those who do not possess such intuitive, prophetic gifts will fail, regardless of how much knowledge they otherwise possess.

Nowadays we are still far removed from emphasizing the prophetic gifts of individuals when training them to become teachers. Indeed, we are nowadays still far removed from a good deal of what will become necessary.[167]

We must become prophets of future humanity if we are to carry out education in the right way. The Greeks were able to rely on instinct, for it was their task to preserve the natural foundations. But as teachers today we must be able to develop Intuition.[168]

In a child's subconscious—and there is infinitely much that lives in the subconscious of a child rather than in his consciousness—a question arises which is not formulated intellectually but lives solely in feelings: Hitherto, self-evident authority has told me what is true, what is good, what is beautiful; this self-evident authority is the embodiment of truth, goodness and beauty; but is this really what it is? There is no need for the doubt to be expressed in words, but it exists. It is present and it enters in the manner described into the life of the child.

Therefore it is necessary, especially regarding this aspect of life—for which one needs to have a healthy, independent gift of observation—to find the right words and the right way to behave. A great deal is necessary. There must be tact, instinct and Intuition. At this point in a child's life one can do something which is of the utmost importance for the entire course of his life on earth. If one finds the remarks, the actions, the relationship through which to show the child: Yes, you are right to regard me as having the necessary authority—then, out of one's inmost soul, one will have become a true benefactor for the child.[169]

Especially in the future one will need something which has been termed, on the one hand very narrow-mindedly but on the other also out of a kind of Intuition, as 'devotion to the trivial'. . . .

You must take into account the difficulty this involves and you must include it in the content of your esoteric striving. You must take account of the tremendous difficulty this involves. An individual who must come to be capable of telling another person something that he knows intuitively . . . needs to be able to say to himself, energetically and courageously, not only in that moment but with it existing constantly and qualitatively within his consciousness: I can do this. If you say this without vanity, and indeed with a willingness to sacrifice, with a willingness to overcome those things which are in opposition to it, if you say this over and over again, and do not merely feel it, then you will come to realize how much you do indeed know in this way. One must search for what is to develop not in a crazy way, not in a fabricated way of thinking but in such a way that one raises up out of one's soul whatever must develop by extricating it in the simplest possible manner from the immense filth, morass or swamp—figuratively speaking—that exists there in one's soul.[170]

Medicine

Today's habits of thought must undergo a radical reversal; and then there will automatically follow an ennobling of feelings and sentiments right up to Intuition. Not until the science of medicine achieves this will it once again contain an element of healing, will something resembling a religious tendency ensoul it, will the physician become what he should be: the noblest friend of humanity who himself feels obliged to raise himself up to such an extent that through his own perfection he is able to carry out his profession in the most elevated manner possible.[171]

The way in which in former times doctors approached their patients was different. It was their intuitive view which they turned not upon what was physical but upon the more delicate, etheric aspect of the physical. Their starting point was: if something is sick, it is less important to look at the externally visible changes than at what has brought these changes about. Disorder in the external physical body matches disorder in the etheric body. The sick organism shows us how the etheric body has been altered and we then aim, through our skills involving medicines, to cure what lies behind the physical body: that which forms, which lies behind the physical body. If I may express this somewhat clumsily: When there is something wrong with a person's stomach, it is not the stomach that is ill but the more subtle body, of which the sickness of the stomach is merely an expression.

Paracelsus had adopted the spirit of medicine that was intuitive in this way. But the authority at that time was the Roman physician Galen. He did indeed tend externally to build his medical practice upon those ancient principles, and when we read superficially what he wrote, we do ask ourselves: Why did Paracelsus battle so strongly against Galen and speak up so forcefully for the ancient ways of medicine? Is that not just the same? Well, it may look as though it is, but actually it is not the same. What Galen made of medicine is a materialistic superficiality, a materialization of a view that was originally spiritual. So Galen's pupils did indeed see something externally materialistic in what had formerly been intuitive. And instead of carrying out their research intuitively they did so merely materialistically while speculating and inventing theories. The moral view had fallen by the wayside.

It was this loss of the intuitive view that Paracelsus rejected. He wanted to return to it, he wanted to find means out of the grandeur of nature which would make it possible to heal the sick. So all that ruled in his day by way of official medical practice was repellent to him. He did not want to base his work on what was written in books; he wanted to open the pages of the great book of nature itself. . . .

He listened to what the simple individual had to say to him. The instinct possessed by the simple individual was for him the Intuition of the genius. He did not cut the cord that bound nature to the original power of Intuition in the human being. . . . What distinguishes Paracelsus is his homogeneous view of the spiritual. Thus the human individual is for him not the one into whom one enters during a physical examination; he is, for him, the one who is bonded entirely with nature as a whole.[172]

What has to happen is that a measure of medical instinct, a measure of medical Intuition—in some cases more like a form of clairvoyance or in others less so—must come about in an individual who becomes an older doctor's assistant. It is then not a question of typically treating matters in a schematic way but rather of working individually in a new way on something previously taught by the older individual—whom one does not merely imitate, but who has trained one and with whom one feels connected.[173]

At the moment when a primeval human being saw something abnormal in an individual he was immediately shown the relevant healing process. This is now lost to modern humanity. Thus a modern individual is less likely to reach through Intuition what, for example, a former individual found through instinct. This is the course of evolution: from instinct via intellectualism to Intuition.[174]

What frequently happens when we imaginatively observe the manifestation of an illness, or indeed any other complex of symptoms, is that we immediately have an intuitive knowledge of the remedy. But then, when we take it for granted that we should consider the matter in connection with what is presented to us in accordance with external, scientific knowledge, we after all think we are mistaken, that it cannot be the case. This is a very common occurrence which comes about in connection not solely with therapeutic matters but altogether with occult investigations. When we then think more carefully about the matter and look into it more thoroughly, we realize that we were right after all. Something which arises out of an imaginative investigation followed by intuitive insight is always right—when it is founded on good powers of knowledge, of course. Nevertheless, our judgement always first has to rise up to an acceptance of the conclusion we have reached in this way. It is indeed necessary to make oneself aware that our human organism is inconceivably complicated, so that reaching an intellectual overview can be exceedingly problematical, especially when we endeavour to see this human organism in connection with the external world.[175]

Eurythmy

In order to give a comprehensive description of what this art of eurythmy really is, what I have to say is: The human being as a whole shall become a metamorphosis of one single organ, an exceedingly lofty and outstanding organ, namely the larynx. Just as the human larynx, through the word and through its sounds, expresses that which lives in the soul, so is it possible, when one intuitively grasps the forces at work in the larynx and in its neighbouring organs by which the sounds and tones are brought forth, to transform these into the forms of movement of the human organism. The entire human organism can become a visible larynx. One must only see clearly, in what the human larynx brings forth by way of words, of sounds, of harmony, of regular sounds and notes, that these are specific movements within the air itself, in which sounds and words are given sense-perceptible, physical expression.

What I would therefore like to say is: That which is formative in the movements which the human larynx sends forth into the air is that which we endeavour to express through the human organism as a whole.[176]

Painting

So the soul of this woman* continued to live within the world of Imagination. And there she encountered another figure, still more strange and more curious than the previous one. Utterly strange and curious. From it flowed something resembling warming love, and also something that could be quite frosty.

'Who are you?' asked the soul of the woman.

'I have a name only over yonder in its right form among those on the physical plane who tell human beings about the spiritual world. Only they know how to apply my name correctly. For my name is Intuition! I am called Intuition and I stem from a vast realm. And through having made my way into the world out of a vast realm I have descended from the region of the Seraphim!'

---

* Rudolf Steiner is describing an allegory in which art is imagined to be the figure of a woman who has various spiritual encounters during clairvoyant sleep.

That figure of Intuition was seraphic in its form. And the soul of the woman asked again: 'What do you wish me to do?'

'You must unite yourself with me! You must have the courage to unite yourself with me! Then will you be able to kindle in the souls of human beings over there on the earth a talent which belongs to their fantasy life through which you will become a part of what just now the youthful messenger described you as.'*

And the soul of the woman decided to do this. And thereby she became something which even in its external form was rather different and rather strange compared with what the external physical human form is and what only someone would have been capable of judging who had looked deep into the human soul. For the soul of the woman had been transformed into what could only be compared with something soul-like, a soul which hitherto still had something etheric about it.

'Because you have done this', said the spiritual, seraphic figure who bore the name of Intuition. 'Because you have done this you can now bring about in human beings the ability to paint artistically. You have become the archetype for painting. Through this you will be able to ignite a talent in human beings. One of their senses, the eye, has something in it untouched by the thinking of the human self, having, on the contrary, the all-inclusive thoughts of the external world. When you have given human beings the creative power of painting you will so enrich the eye that this sense will

---

* The figure of the woman had heard from the youthful messenger, who had been born out of the shine of the red of evening, the words: 'You are art!' (GA 271).

recognize soul existence in what is otherwise soulless and inanimate, known only from its surface. Human beings will ensoul all that on the surface appears as colour and form, so handling it that the form will tell of the soul. And through the colours something will speak that is not only outwardly perceptible, but human beings will enchant into the field of colours the language of the colours themselves, telling of their inner nature, just as all that comes from me passes from inner being to outer appearance. You will give human beings a capacity enabling them by their own soul's light to carry the soul's power of movement into the lifeless world, into otherwise soulless colours and forms. Through your gift they will transform movement into stillness, they will hold fast what in the outer world is in continually changing movement. The briefly fleeting colours, touched by the rising sun, the colours of lifeless nature, these you will teach them to hold fast!'[177]

Notes

For consistency of language and style, German texts from Rudolf Steiner have been translated afresh. Thus, page references refer to the German editions, as published by Rudolf Steiner Verlag, Switzerland. However, published English translations of complete volumes, listed by the Collected Works ('GA') number are given on page 136.

1. GA 1, quoted from J.W.Goethe: *Schriften zur Botanik und Wissenschaftslehre* with a postscript by A.B.Wachsmuth, Munich 1975.
2. GA 1.
3. GA 38. Letter to Eduard von Hartmann, 4 September 1884.
4. GA 1, *Einleitungen zu Goethes Naturwissenschaftlichen Schriften, 1884.*
5. Ibid.
6. Ibid.
7. GA 2, *Grundlinien einer Erkenntnistheorie, 1886.*
8. Ibid.
9. Ibid.
10. Ibid.
11. Ibid.
12. Ibid.
13. Ibid.
14. GA 1, *Einleitungen zu Goethes Naturwissenschaftlichen Schriften, 1884.*
15. Ibid.
16. GA 6, *Goethes Weltanschauung, 1897.*

17. GA 34, lecture September 1905.
18. GA 51, lecture Berlin, 4 February 1905.
19. GA 53, lecture Berlin, 9 February 1905.
20. Ibid., lecture Berlin, 16 February 1905.
21. GA 35, lecture London, 10 July 1905.
22. Ibid.
23. GA 55, lecture Berlin, 14 February 1907.
24. GA 125, lecture Leipzig, 21 November 1910.
25. GA 129, lecture Munich, 28 August 1911.
26. GA 185, lecture Dornach, 1 November 1918.
27. GA 277, lecture Zürich, 24 February 1919.
28. GA 312, lecture Dornach, 30 March 1920.
29. GA 4.
30. Ibid.
31. Ibid.
32. Ibid.
33. Ibid.
34. Ibid.
35. Ibid.
36. Ibid.
37. Ibid.
38. Ibid.
39. GA 34, essay *Charakteristik von Paul Asmus' Weltanschauung, 1904.*
40. GA 18.
41. GA 51, lecture Berlin, 7 May 1902.
42. GA 152, lecture Stuttgart, 5 March 1914.
43. GA 185, lectures Dornach, 27 October 1918 and 26 October 1918.
44. GA 189, lecture Dornach, 16 March 1919.
45. GA 255b, lecture Dornach, 16 November 1919. In his article

'Rudolf Steiner als Philosoph und Theosoph', (Tübingen 1919/1921), German theology professor Friedrich Traub (1860–1939) criticized Anthroposophy as being incompatible with the Christian faith.

46. GA 333, lecture Stuttgart, 19 December 1919.

47. Ibid.

48. GA 333, lecture Stuttgart, 30 December 1919.

49. GA 335, lecture Stuttgart, 15 June 1920.

50. Ibid.

51. GA 205, lecture Berne, 28 June 1921.

52. Ibid.

53. GA 9.

54. Ibid.

55. Ibid.

56. GA 98, lecture Berlin, 26 May 1904.

57. GA 93a, lecture Berlin, 12 October 1905.

58. Ibid.

59. GA 324a, lecture Berlin, 7 November 1905.

60. GA 54, lecture Berlin, 26 April 1906.

61. GA 115, lecture Berlin, 26 October 1909.

62. GA 145, lecture The Hague, 29 March 1913.

63. Ibid.

64. Ibid.

65. GA 151, lecture Berlin, 22 January 1914.

66. GA 293, lecture Stuttgart, 27 August 1919.

67. GA 324, lecture Stuttgart, 23 March 1921.

68. Ibid.

69. Ibid.

70. GA 84, lecture Dornach, 14 April 1923.

71. GA 236, lecture Dornach, 10 May 1924.

72. Ibid.

73. GA 34, The Theosophical Congress in Amsterdam, June 1904.

74. GA 12.

75. Ibid.

76. Ibid.

77. Ibid.

78. Ibid.

79. Ibid.

80. Ibid.

81. GA 13.

82. Ibid.

83. Ibid.

84. Ibid.

85. GA 27.

86. GA 35, essay 'Die psychologischen Grundlagen und die erkenntnistheoretische Stellung der Anthroposophie', 1911.

87. Ibid., essay 'Frühere Geheimhaltung und jetzige Veröffentlichung übersinnlicher Erkenntnisse, 1918.

88. GA 51, lecture Berlin, 5 November 1904.

89. GA 93, lecture Berlin, 2 December 1904.

90. GA 89, lecture Berlin, 3 April 1905.

91. GA 35, lecture Paris, 4 June 1906.

92. GA 99, lecture Munich, 25 May 1907.

93. GA 105, lecture Stuttgart, 12 August 1908.

94. GA 62, lecture Berlin, 21 November 1912.

95. Ibid.

96. GA 63, lecture Berlin, 20 November 1913.

97. GA 168, lecture Berne, 9 November 1916.

98. GA 324, lecture Stuttgart, 23 March 1921.

99. GA 303, lecture Dornach, 27 December 1921.

100. GA 215, lecture Dornach, 7 September 1922.

101. Ibid.

102. GA 84, lecture Paris, 26 May 1924.

103. GA 12.

104. GA 13.

105. Ibid.

106. GA 25.

107. Ibid.

108. Ibid.

109. Ibid.

110. GA 59, lecture Berlin, 10 February 1910.

111. GA 62, lecture Berlin, 3 April 1913.

112. Ibid.

113. GA 63, lecture Berlin, 27 November 1913.

114. GA 153, lecture Vienna, 6 April 1914.

115. Ibid.

116. GA 324, lecture Stuttgart, 23 March 1921.

117. GA 12.

118. GA 13.

119. Ibid.

120. GA 25.

121. GA 35, essay 'Meine "Zustimmung" zu Richard Wahles "Erkenntniskritik und Anthroposophie",' 1923.

122. GA 260a, lecture Prague, 13 April 1924.

123. GA 56, lecture Berlin, 10 October 1907.

124. GA 266a, Esoteric Lesson Berlin, 1 November 1907.

125. GA 110, lecture Düsseldorf, 12 April 1909.

126. GA 113, lecture Munich, 31 August 1909.

127. GA 58, lecture Berlin, 14 October 1909.

128. GA 115, lecture Berlin, 15 December 1911.

129. GA 134, lecture Hanover, 30 December 1911.

130. GA 134, lecture Hanover, 1 January 1912.

131. GA 61, lecture Berlin, 15 February 1912.

132. GA 61, lecture Berlin, 28 March 1912.

133. GA 141, lecture Berlin, 5 November 1912.

134. GA 62, lecture Berlin, 21 November 1912.

135. GA 179, lecture Dornach, 15 December 1917.

136. GA 181, lecture Berlin, 6 August 1918.

137. GA 188, lecture Dornach, 11 January 1919.

138. GA 322, lecture Dornach, 2 October 1920.

139. GA 291, lecture Dornach, 5 December 1920.

140. GA 255b, lecture Stuttgart, 25 May 1921.

141. GA 303, lecture Dornach, 26 December 1921.

142. GA 304, lecture Stratford-on-Avon, 23 April 1922.

143. GA 239, lecture Paris, 23 May 1924.

144. GA 346, lecture Dornach, 7 September 1924.

145. GA 13.

146. GA 35, essay 'Die Erkenntnis vom Zustand zwischen dem Tode und einer neuen Geburt', 1916.

147. Ibid.

148. GA 25.

149. Ibid.

150. GA 26.

151. GA 181, lecture Berlin, 2 April 1918.

152. GA 174b, lecture Stuttgart, 23 April 1918.

153. GA 174a, lecture Munich, 4 May 1918.

154. GA 82, lecture The Hague, 12 April 1922.

155. GA 215, lecture Dornach, 9 September 1922.

156. GA 231, lecture The Hague, 13 November 1923.

157. GA 234, lecture Dornach, 3 February 1924.

158. GA 324a, lecture Stuttgart, 11 March 1920.

159. GA 93, lecture Berlin, 2 December 1904.

160. GA 276, lecture Dornach, 1 June 1923.

161. GA 328, lecture Zürich, 10 February 1919.

162. GA 190, lecture Dornach, 29 March 1919.

163. GA 296, lecture Dornach, 9 August 1919.

164. GA 296, lecture Dornach, 11 August 1919.

165. Ibid.

166. GA 55, lecture Cologne, 1 December 1906.

167. GA 177, lecture Dornach, 8 October 1917.

168. GA 307, lecture Ilkley, 7 August 1923.

169. GA 298, lecture Stuttgart, 1 June 1924.

170. GA 317, lecture Dornach, 5 July 1924.

171. GA 53, lecture Berlin, 25 May 1905

172. GA 54, lecture Berlin, 26 April 1906.

173. GA 192, lecture Stuttgart, 3 August 1919.

174. GA 312, lecture Dornach, 4 April 1920.

175. GA 313, lecture Dornach, 16 April 1921.

176. GA 277, lecture Zürich, 24 February 1919.

177. GA 271, lecture Berlin, 28 October 1909.

Sources

The following volumes are cited in this book. Where relevant, published editions of equivalent English translations are provided.

The works of Rudolf Steiner are listed with the volume numbers of the complete works in German, the *Gesamtausgabe* (GA), as published by Rudolf Steiner Verlag, Dornach, Switzerland.

GA

1   *Nature's Open Secret*

2   *Goethe's Theory of Knowledge*

4   *The Philosophy of Freedom, The Basis for a Modern World Conception* (8th English edition, 2011)

6   *Goethe's World View*

9   *Theosophy*

10   *Knowledge of the Higher Worlds*

12   *Stages of Higher Knowledge*

13   *An Outline of Esoteric Science/Occult Science: an Outline*

14   *Four Mystery Plays*

16   *A Way of Self-Knowledge*

18   *Riddles of Philosophy*

23   *Towards Social Renewal*

25   *Cosmology*

26   *Anthroposophical Leading Thoughts*

27   *Extending Practical Medicine*

34   *Lucifer-Gnosis. Grundlegende Aufsätze zur Anthroposophie 1903–1908*

35   *Philosophie und Anthroposophie. Gesammelte Aufsätze 1904– 1923*

138   INTUITION